AF507248

52-Week Bible Study for Families Made Simple

Weekly Lessons, Guided Questions, and Prayers to Grow in Faith Together

Welcome Aboard, Check Out This Limited-Time Free Bonus!

Ahoy, reader! Welcome to the Ahoy Publications family, and thanks for snagging a copy of this book! Since you've chosen to join us on this journey, we'd like to offer you something special.

Check out the link below for a FREE e-book filled with delightful facts about American History.

But that's not all - you'll also have access to our exclusive email list with even more free e-books and insider knowledge. Well, what are ye waiting for? Click the link below to join and set sail toward exciting adventures in American History.

Access your bonus here

https://ahoypublications.com/

Or, Scan the QR code!

Table of Contents

Introduction

You probably didn't plan for this to feel hard. You wanted faith in your home to be natural, not forced.

Weeks pass quickly. Days fill up. And even when you care, it's easy for Scripture to get pushed aside. This isn't because you've failed. It's because no habit grows on its own.

In most families, no one announces, "We'll stop reading the Bible now." It's quieter than that. One week gets skipped. Then another. Maybe you try to restart, but the moment feels stiff or unsure. It feels like starting over. That's where this book helps. Not with big commitments, but with small, steady ones that return each week.

This study gives your family a rhythm. One passage. One teaching. A few questions. A short prayer. That's it. You meet once a week, and the pattern repeats. But the words change. The verse changes. And slowly, the habit starts to shape your home.

You won't need to explain everything. You won't need to lead like a pastor. You'll need to show up, open your Bible, read what's there, and listen. Children notice patterns more than they notice perfect words. They hear if your voice is calm or rushed. They see if the Bible stays closed. They pick up on what matters by what returns week after week.

This study was written for real homes. Not quiet ones. Not ones where kids sit still the whole time. It's for tables where people shift in their seats. Where one child mumbles an answer and another asks something completely off-topic. That's part of the point. Faith grows in regular houses with regular families.

You don't have to create the change. That's not your job. You are creating space. God does the work. If He isn't building the house, no structure will hold. But if you give Him space, even twenty minutes a week, you will see something take root.

How to Use This Study as a Family

Pick one day. Keep it the same each week if you can. Most families do well with Sunday evening or a weekday night after dinner. Let everyone know this is a time that matters. Try not to move it around.

Start with the Bible passage. Read it out loud. Don't rush. If your kids can read, let them take turns.

Next, read the short lesson. One person can read it aloud, or everyone can read silently. Sit together. Avoid phones. It helps to use the same Bible each week.

Then move into the questions. Let each person answer in their own way. There's no need to explain everything. Keep the conversation natural.

End with prayer. One person can pray, or several can share short prayers. Don't overthink it.

If you miss a week, skip ahead. Don't double up. Don't quit. Keep going.

Building a Weekly Faith Habit

Twenty to thirty minutes once a week. That's all this takes. Over time, it builds something strong. Faith doesn't grow through perfect speeches. It grows through regular time with God's Word.

Use the same space in your home each week. Keep a Bible there. Keep it simple. Stay patient. Missed weeks don't break the pattern. Showing up again does.

Start now. Not once everything's perfect. Not once everyone's "ready." God meets families who make room for Him, even in the middle of a noisy, normal evening.

Part 1: Foundations of Faith

Week 1: Trust in God's Plan

"Trust in the Lord with all your heart, and do not lean on your own understanding. In all your ways acknowledge Him, and He will make straight your paths". - Proverbs 3:5-6

Trust is hard to teach, especially when you struggle with it yourself. You want your children to believe God will take care of them, but life offers a hundred chances a week to doubt. Problems come up. Plans change. Things feel uncertain. When that happens, the question becomes simple: who are you leaning on?

This verse does not ask for half your heart. It asks for all of it. Trust in the Lord with all your heart. That includes the part that wants to solve everything alone. That includes the part that feels confused when the outcome isn't clear. God does not ask you to understand. He asks you to trust.

Leaning on your own understanding feels natural. It gives you a sense of control. It also brings stress. It causes fear. It puts too much weight on your shoulders. When you trust in God's plan, that weight shifts. You don't stop thinking. You stop depending on your own wisdom to hold everything together.

"In all your ways acknowledge Him." That means you don't separate your faith from your schedule, your money, or your parenting. You bring God into every part of your life. You speak His name aloud. You make space to pray when things feel too small to matter. You say, "God, I need help here." And He responds.

He may not respond how or when you want, but He does not ignore His people. "He will make straight your paths" does not mean the road will be easy. It means He will guide it. You won't have to walk in circles. He will lead you forward. Step by step.

This week, think about one area where your family feels stuck or uncertain. Don't explain it away. Don't rush to solve it. Acknowledge it in prayer. Out loud. Together. Then ask God to make your path straight in that specific area. Trust Him with it fully, even if you don't understand how He'll answer.

Discussion Questions

1. What does it mean to trust God with all your heart?
2. Where are you tempted to lean on your own understanding?
3. What does acknowledging God look like on a normal day?
4. How can your family trust Him together this week?

Family Prayer

God, we admit we don't always trust You. We try to fix things on our own. We worry about what's ahead. Help us give You our full hearts, not just the easy parts. Teach us to lean on You and not on ourselves. Remind us to include You in our decisions, our fears, and our plans. Lead us on the path You've prepared, even when we can't see where it leads. We want to follow You. In Jesus' name. Amen.

Week 2: The Power of Prayer

"Do not be anxious about anything, but in everything by prayer and supplication with thanksgiving let your requests be made known to God." - Philippians 4:6

Anxiety comes fast. It shows up in the middle of the night. It shows up during meals. It shows up when something feels too big to fix or too uncertain to understand. God does not ignore this. He gives a clear answer, and it is not complicated. When you feel anxious, pray.

Prayer is not a last resort. It is the first thing God tells us to do. Talk to Him. Tell Him what is wrong. Ask Him for help. Use normal words. You don't need a special language. You don't need a plan. You need to speak honestly to the God who already knows what you're going through.

The verse says, "in everything by prayer." That means the small stuff, too. The test at school. The lost keys. The car repair. The child who won't sleep. The fear that keeps coming back. If it makes you anxious, it belongs in prayer. God does not rank your problems. He receives them all.

"By prayer and supplication." Supplication means asking for what you need. You are not bothering God when you ask. You are not being selfish. You are doing what He told you to do. He is not tired of hearing your voice.

"With thanksgiving." This part matters. You don't have to feel thankful to say thank you. You can thank God for being near. You can thank Him for hearing you. You can thank Him for staying the same when everything else changes. Gratitude pulls your eyes off the problem and places them back on God.

"Let your requests be made known to God." He already knows what you need, but He still tells you to bring it to Him. Why? Because trust grows through communication. Children know this with their parents. The talking itself builds connection. God wants your requests because He wants your heart.

Families that pray out loud grow closer, not because their prayers are perfect, but because they practice trust together. If something makes your child anxious, stop and pray with them. If something is bothering you, tell your family and ask them to pray with you. Keep it short. Keep it real.

Prayer will not remove every problem, but it will remind your family that they are not alone in facing them. This week, decide as a family to pray before acting when something causes stress. Pause, even for one minute, and speak to God. Make it a habit.

Discussion Questions

1. What makes you anxious right now?
2. Do you usually pray first, or do you try to fix things first?
3. How does giving thanks during prayer change your attitude?
4. How can we help each other remember to pray this week?

Family Prayer

Father, thank You for listening when we pray. We worry about many things. Some are big, some are small, but they all affect our hearts. Teach us to pray about everything, not just emergencies. Help us bring our requests to You and trust that You hear. Remind us to give thanks, even when things feel hard. We want to be a family that turns to You first. In Jesus' name,. Amen.

Week 3: God's Word in Your Home

"Your word is a lamp to my feet and a light to my path." - Psalm 119:105

Most days feel full before they even start. You wake up, and the list is already waiting. Meals to make. School to get through. Work to finish. Tasks to remember. Evenings disappear. Time gets used up fast. It's easy to say the Bible matters. It's harder to make space for it.

This verse reminds us why God's Word isn't optional. It lights the path. It shows what comes next. Without it, you're walking in the dark. You might still move forward, but you're guessing. You're making choices with unclear direction. God does not want that for you or your children.

His Word lights the next step, not the whole road. It may not give you every answer at once, but it gives you enough for now. That's how God works. He gives light as you walk. When you stay in Scripture, you stay in the light.

Many homes say they believe in the Bible but treat it like a backup tool. It sits unopened. It comes out during crisis or special events, but this verse tells us it's daily equipment. A lamp is no use if it stays off. A light must be turned on to help.

When God's Word is part of your home life, your family sees that truth matters. Decisions don't have to be guesses. God speaks through His Word, and He has already told us the kind of life He blesses. Children need to hear it. Parents need it too.

Reading the Bible does not need to take hours. It needs to happen often. Keep one Bible where your family meets. Open it out loud, even if it's only one passage. Let your children hear it spoken. Let them read it with you. When questions come up, don't rush to explain. Read again. Let the words work.

When you make space for God's Word in your house, you make space for wisdom. You show your children where to go for direction when things feel unclear. You also remind yourself that God does not leave His people guessing. He speaks, and His Word lights the path.

This week, pick one time in the day besides this study to open the Bible together. It could be before school, after dinner, or right before bed. Choose one short passage and read it as a family. Say nothing else if needed. The reading itself builds the habit.

Discussion Questions

1. What happens when we try to make decisions without God's Word?
2. How does Scripture help us take the next right step?
3. Is the Bible visible and active in our home? If not, how can that change?
4. What time of day would work best for short family Scripture reading?

Family Prayer

God, thank You for giving us Your Word. We forget how much we need it. Sometimes we try to figure things out on our own. Sometimes we walk forward without asking what You've already said. Help us turn to Scripture first. Show us how to build this habit in our home. Give us light for today and teach us to trust You with the rest. In Jesus' name. Amen.

Week 4: Walking in Obedience

"If you love me, keep my commands." - John 14:15

It's easy to say you love God. It's harder to show it when you're tired, frustrated, or when doing what's right costs you something. Jesus doesn't say, "If you love me, you'll talk about it." He says, "You'll obey me." That's a strong statement, but it's simple. Love for God shows up in what you do, not just what you say.

Obedience isn't about trying to earn God's favor. You already have His love. Obedience is a response. When you love someone, you want to honor what matters to them. You listen. You adjust. You pay attention. In the same way, when your heart is turned toward God, you care about His words.

For children, the idea of obedience usually starts with rules. "Do this. Don't do that."

Jesus ties obedience to love, not rules. That changes the tone. It's not fear-based. It's not about control. It's about trust. You trust that His commands are good, even when they're hard.

This doesn't mean it always feels easy. Sometimes obedience is choosing to be quiet when you want to speak. Sometimes it's being kind when someone else is rude. Other times it means forgiving, even when you don't feel like it. These are not small things. And they are not natural, but they are part of following Jesus.

In a home, obedience to God gets tested all the time. One child pushes another. Parents lose patience. Words are said in a rush. The test isn't whether your family never struggles. The question is: what do you do next? Do you come back to what God says? Do you teach your kids that obedience is still the goal, even after failure?

Children learn best from what they see. If they watch their parents obey God in real situations, they'll understand this better than if they hear a lecture. If you make a mistake and say, "That wasn't what God wants. I need to make it right," that speaks louder than rules ever could.

Jesus wants your obedience because He wants your heart. He knows that following His commands will lead to peace, even when it costs something in the short term. He's not trying to control you. He's trying to protect you.

This week, choose one thing your family can do to obey God more closely. Keep it simple. Maybe it's using kind words during conflict. Maybe it's praying for someone instead of complaining about them. One small act of obedience can reset the tone in your home.

Discussion Questions

1. What does obedience to God look like in daily life?
2. Why does Jesus connect love with keeping His commands?
3. When is it hardest for you to obey?
4. What is one small way we can obey God better this week?

Family Prayer

Jesus, thank You for showing us how to live. You obeyed the Father perfectly, and You ask us to follow You. We admit that we don't always get it right. Help us care about what You say. Help us show our love for You by doing what You've told us to do. Give us strength when obedience feels hard. Teach us to follow You in our home, our words, and our actions. In Your name we pray. Amen.

Week 5: Living with Gratitude

"Give thanks in all circumstances; for this is the will of God in Christ Jesus for you." - 1 Thessalonians 5:18

Some days it's easy to say thank you. The sun is out, everyone's in a good mood, and things are going the way you hoped. Other days, it's not easy at all. A plan falls apart. Someone gets sick. A child acts out. In those moments, gratitude feels far away.

But God doesn't tell us to give thanks *for* every situation. He tells us to give thanks *in* every situation. That's a difference worth noticing. You don't have to pretend bad things are good. You don't have to enjoy what hurts. Even in hard times, you can still look for reasons to thank God.

Why? Because gratitude keeps your heart pointed in the right direction. Without it, frustration takes over. You start to focus only on what's missing. You miss the quiet ways God is still working, but when you stop, even briefly, to thank Him, something shifts.

Paul wrote this verse from experience. He was no stranger to hardship. He was beaten, arrested, and rejected. Still, he wrote to the church and told them to be thankful in all circumstances. This wasn't a suggestion. It was God's will for them. And for us.

In a home, the mood often follows what's being said out loud. If complaints lead the conversation, the whole house feels heavier. If someone gives thanks, even in a small way, it lifts the tone. Gratitude doesn't fix problems, but it changes how you carry them.

Children watch how their parents respond to hard days. They hear how you talk about work, finances, interruptions, and one another. If they see thankfulness in you, even when things are hard, they learn that joy and gratitude aren't based on comfort.

One of the best ways to train your family in gratitude is to build it into your normal routine. It doesn't have to be formal. You can ask, "What's one thing you're thankful for today?" at the dinner table. You can say, "God, thank You for this food" and mean it. You can thank God when plans do work out and also when they don't.

Gratitude doesn't mean you avoid honest feelings. It means you tell the truth while still trusting God. You can say, "This was a hard day, but God gave us strength to get through it." That's real. That's what your children need to hear.

This week, be the one in your home who starts the habit of giving thanks out loud. Even one sentence can change the direction of a moment. Gratitude teaches your family to look for God's presence, not just His blessings.

Discussion Questions

1. Why do you think God wants us to give thanks in all situations?
2. What's the difference between giving thanks for something and giving thanks during something?
3. How does gratitude affect the mood of your home?
4. What is one way we can practice thankfulness this week?

Family Prayer

God, we don't always feel thankful. Sometimes we forget to stop and recognize what You've done. Help us notice Your care, even on ordinary days. Remind us to say thank You, not just when things go well, but all the time. Build a grateful spirit in our home. Teach us to speak thankfulness out loud. We want our hearts to stay turned toward You. In Jesus' name. Amen.

Week 6: Faith Over Fear

"Don't be afraid, for I am with you. Don't be discouraged, for I am your God. I will strengthen you and help you. I will hold you up with my victorious right hand." - Isaiah 41:10

Fear speaks in quick thoughts. Fear pushes you to react. Fear tells you to protect yourself first. In a family, fear often shows up as anger, silence, control, or worry. You feel pressure to keep everyone safe and steady. When fear leads, your home feels tense.

God gives clear words. Do not be afraid, for I am with you. God does not offer a trick to remove fear. God offers His presence. You are not facing trouble by yourself. God stays near in hard moments, in loud rooms, and in quiet nights.

Fear pulls your focus from God and toward self.

Fear often grows when you feel alone. You look at bills, health, school problems, or conflict, then you start to plan without prayer. You start to carry weight God never asked you to carry. This verse calls you to stop and look up. God says, "I am with you." Say those words out loud when fear rises. Teach your children to say them too.

God also says, "I am your God." Fear makes you forget who leads. You belong to the Lord. You answer to Him, not to your feelings. Fear does not rule your choices. God rules your life. This changes how you respond. You slow down. You speak with care. You choose obedience over panic.

The verse gives four promises. God will strengthen you. God will help you. God will hold you up. God will use His right hand, not your strength. Your job is faith, not control. You take steps God asks for. You rest from trying to manage every outcome.

Practice this as a family. Name one fear each person carries this week. Keep names simple. Speak them without drama. Then pray over each one. Ask God for strength and help. Next, choose one action step. If fear comes from money, plan one wise change. If fear comes from conflict, plan one hard talk with calm words. If fear comes from school, plan one study block and one prayer. Keep actions small and clear.

Also train your words. When a child says, "I am scared," do not shut down the feeling. Guide the child to truth. Say, "God is with you." Say, "God will help you." Then ask, "What next step will you take with God beside you?" Fear shrinks when faith moves.

This week, watch your own patterns. When stress hits, do you rush, blame, or withdraw. Stop early. Take a slow breath. Pray one sentence. Then act with steady hands. Faith over fear starts with small choices made on purpose.

Discussion Questions

1. Where do you feel fear most often as a family?
2. What signs show fear has started to lead?
3. What does God's presence change in your response?
4. What one action step will you take this week when fear rises?

Family Prayer

Father, fear pulls our minds in many directions. Bring us back to Your words. You are with us. You are our God. Strengthen us when we feel weak. Help us when we feel stuck. Hold us up when we feel tired. Teach us to act with faith and calm. Give our home peace through trust in Jesus. Amen.

Week 7: Loving God Fully

"Love the Lord your God with all your heart and with all your soul and with all your strength." - Deuteronomy 6:5

God calls for full love. Not part. Not leftover. Love starts inside. Heart means your desires and choices. Soul means your life and identity. Strength means your effort, time, and energy. God does not ask for words only. God asks for a whole life.

Start with your heart. What do you want most. What do you chase when no one watches? What do you protect? If your heart runs toward comfort, praise, or control, your love for God weakens. You correct this through repentance. You name the wrong desire. You turn from it. You choose obedience.

Next is your soul. Your soul belongs to God. Your family roles matter, yet they do not define you most. Your job title does not define you most. God does. When you remember this, you stop living for approval. You stop fearing people. You live to please God.

Then strength. Love uses hands and feet. You show love for God through actions. You show love through worship, prayer, service, and giving. You show love through how you speak at home. You show love through what you allow on screens. You show love through how you spend money.

Loving God fully starts with simple habits.

Set a daily time for the Word. Pick one time and protect it. Ten minutes works. Read one passage. Ask two questions. What does God say? What will I obey today? Write one sentence. Do not aim for volume. Aim for faithfulness.

Pray in short sentences throughout the day. Pray when you wake up. Pray before meals. Pray before hard talks. Pray before sleep. Keep prayers plain. Thank God. Confess sin. Ask for help. Ask for wisdom.

Practice worship at home. Sing one song. Read one Psalm. Say one verse out loud. Let children see parents worship. Let children hear parents ask forgiveness.

Teach love through choices. If your family schedule leaves no time for God, change it. If screens steal attention, set limits. If tiredness leads to harsh words, plan rest and quiet. If money drives stress, build a simple budget and give on purpose. Obedience often starts with planning.

Love also shapes discipline. When you correct a child, your goal is not control. Your goal is love for God. Explain why obedience matters. Connect choices to God's commands. Use clear consequences. Use calm words. Then pray with the child.

Love shapes conflict too. When you argue, ask one question. "What response shows love for God right now." This question slows anger. This question lifts your eyes.

Make one family practice for this week. Each person names one way to love God with heart, one with soul, one with strength. Keep answers practical. Then choose one action for each person. Write the actions down. Review them at the end of the week.

Love grows through repetition. You choose God again and again. When you fail, you return fast. You confess. You change direction. You keep moving.

Discussion Questions

1. What pulls your heart away from God?
2. How do you show love for God with your choices?
3. What action will you take this week to love God with strength?
4. What change will help your family put God first?

Family Prayer

Lord God, You deserve our whole love. Turn our hearts toward You. Help us belong to You in every part of life. Give us strength to obey. Teach our family to love You first each day. Forgive our divided hearts. Lead us in faithful steps. Amen.

Week 8: Teaching Your Children Diligently

"Repeat them again and again to your children. Talk about them when you are at home and when you are on the road, when you are going to bed and when you are getting up." - Deuteronomy 6:7

God gives parents a clear task. Teach His words to your children. Not once in a while. Not only at church. Not only when trouble hits. Teach through steady repetition. Teach through normal life.

This verse points to a pattern. Home. Road. Bed. Morning. God's Word belongs in every part of family life. Teaching does not need long lessons. Teaching needs faithfulness. Short moments add up.

Start with repeat. Children learn through hearing the same truth many times. You repeat because hearts drift. You repeat because attention fades. You repeat because God's commands shape choices. Repetition builds memory. Memory builds habits. Habits shape character.

Use the moments named in the verse.

At home. Choose one daily anchor time. Dinner works well. Read one verse or one short passage. Ask one question. "What does God want us to do?" Then each person answers in one sentence. Keep it focused. End with a short prayer.

On the road. Use travel time for talking. Ask one simple question. "Where did you see God's kindness today?" Or, "What choice do you need wisdom for tomorrow?" Keep it light, yet serious. Listen more than you speak. Help your children connect life to God's truth.

Going to bed. Bedtime is a strong moment. Fear and guilt often rise at night. Read a few lines of Scripture. Ask, "Do you need to confess anything to God?" Then pray. Bless your child with one sentence. "The Lord is with you." Keep it calm.

Getting up. Mornings set direction. Speak one truth before the day begins. Put a verse on the fridge. Say it together. Pray for one need for each person. Then step into the day with purpose.

Diligent teaching also means you plan.

Pick one theme for the week. Obedience. Truth. Kindness. Courage. Use one passage connected to the theme. Refer to it during the week. When a moment comes, link back to the theme. Do not lecture. Point. Ask. Guide.

Use clear language. Children need direct words. Say, "God tells us to tell the truth." Say, "God tells us to forgive." Avoid long speeches. Give one reason. "We obey because we love God." Then give one step.

Model the message. Teaching without example loses force. If you tell your children to pray, let them see you pray. If you teach forgiveness, ask forgiveness when you sin. If you teach self control, show calm when stressed. Your life is part of the lesson.

Correct with Scripture. When a child disobeys, connect the issue to God's Word. Say, "God tells us to honor." Then apply a clear consequence. Be steady. Do not threaten. Do not bargain. After correction, restore with love. Pray together. Move forward.

Invite questions. Children will ask hard things. Do not fear questions. Say, "Let's look at what Scripture says." If you do not know, say, "I will find the answer." Then follow through. This builds trust.

This week, set one simple goal. Use Deuteronomy 6:7 each day in one daily moment. Track it on a paper chart. Keep the goal small. Keep it steady. Diligence grows through routine.

Discussion Questions

1. Which daily moment is easiest for Bible talk?
2. Which daily moment is hardest?
3. What topic does your family need to learn this week?
4. What one habit will help you teach with consistency?

Family Prayer

Lord, thank You for Your Word. Help us teach it with faithfulness. Give us simple words and steady habits. Help our children hear the truth often and follow You with joy. Forgive our neglect and our distraction. Build a home shaped by Scripture. Amen.

Week 9: Building on the Rock

"Anyone who listens to my teaching and follows it is wise, like a person who builds a house on solid rock." - Matthew 7:24

Jesus links wisdom to action. You hear His words, then you obey. Many families hear the truth on Sunday, then forget on Monday. This week calls you to change your routine. Listening without obedience leaves your home fragile under pressure.

Start with one clear rule. In your home, Scripture leads decisions. Feelings do not lead. Opinions do not lead. When a choice appears, you pause. You ask, "What did Jesus teach?" Then you act on His teaching.

Obedience needs a plan. Pick one area where your family struggles. Choose one. Speech. Time. Money. Screen use. Respect. Truthfulness. Forgiveness. Write a simple family agreement for seven days. Keep words short. Make each rule measurable.

Example: Speech. Rule: No shouting. No insults. No sarcasm. When anger rises, take a two minute pause, then speak again with calm words.

Example: Time. Rule: Ten minutes of Bible reading each day after dinner, before any entertainment.

Example: Screen use. Rule: Devices stay out of bedrooms. Screens stop one hour before sleep.

After you choose one rule, connect obedience to Jesus. Say, "We obey because Jesus speaks with authority." Then follow through with steady practice. Do not threaten. Do not bargain. Set a consequence ahead of time. Use calm correction.

Building on solid rock also means you prepare before trouble arrives. You teach your children to obey in small things. You train habits when life feels normal. When crisis hits, habits hold. Without habits, fear drives choices.

Use a daily check in. Each night, each person answers two questions. "Where did I obey Jesus today?" "Where did I refuse obedience?" Keep answers brief. No speeches. Parents answer too. End with confession and one next step.

Set one weekly family meeting. Review the rule. Celebrate wins. Admit failures. Change consequences. Pray together. Keep the meeting under fifteen minutes.

Keep your focus on hearing and doing. Hearing means you open Scripture. You read. You listen. You talk about meaning. Doing so means you change behavior. You speak a hard apology. You return stolen property. You end a dishonest habit. You keep a promise. You tell the truth even when consequences hurt.

Expect resistance. Your own heart resists obedience. Your children resist limits. Stay steady. Do not argue for hours. State the rule. Apply the consequence. Offer a path back through repentance and repair.

Use a simple repair practice. When someone breaks the rule, three steps follow. First, admit wrong. Second, ask forgiveness. Third, make one concrete repair. Replace, return, redo, or serve. Then move forward.

This week, mark progress. Put a paper on the fridge. Each day, record one act of obedience for each person. Keep entries short. One sentence each. At the end of seven days, read the list aloud. Thank God for growth. Choose one habit to keep.

Discussion Questions

1. What teaching of Jesus do you find hardest to obey?
2. What rule will help your family obey for seven days?
3. What consequence will you use when someone refuses the rule?
4. What repair step helps restore trust after disobedience?

Family Prayer

Lord Jesus, You speak truth. Help us listen and obey. Show each of us one step for today. Give us self control. Give us courage to repent fast. Build our home on obedience to Your words. Amen.

Week 10: The Joy of Salvation

"If you openly declare that Jesus is Lord and believe in your heart that God raised him from the dead, you will be saved." - Romans 10:9

Salvation brings joy because God rescues you from sin and death. Joy grows when you remember what God did, what God promised, and how you respond each day. This week focuses on one clear truth. God saves through Jesus.

Romans 10:9 gives two responses. Confess with your mouth. Believe in your heart. Both matter. Confession means you speak agreement with God. Jesus is Lord. Lord means Jesus rules. Jesus leads. Jesus owns every part of life. Belief means trust from the inner person. God raised Jesus from the dead. Resurrection proves victory over sin. Resurrection proves Jesus speaks with authority. Resurrection gives hope beyond the grave.

Confession without belief turns into empty words. Belief without confession stays hidden. God calls for faith with words. A home needs faith with words too.

Start with personal clarity. Write one sentence. "Jesus is Lord of my life." Say this sentence out loud each morning for seven days. Do not rush. Speak with focus. Then pray one request. "Lord Jesus, lead my choices today."

Next, name what salvation means. Salvation includes forgiveness. God removes guilt through the cross. Salvation includes a new standing with God. God accepts you through Jesus. Salvation includes a new direction. You turn from sin. You follow Christ. Salvation includes a new future.

Eternal life begins now and continues after death.

Bring this truth into family talk. Choose one meal this week for a salvation conversation. Parents speak first. Share how Jesus saved you. Use plain words. Keep details age appropriate. Speak facts. Speak changes. Speak gratitude. Children learn through hearing real stories.

Ask each child one question. "Who is Jesus to you?" Listen. If a child shows confusion, guide with Scripture, not pressure. Read Romans 10:9 again. Explain each phrase. Jesus is Lord. God raised Jesus. Saved means rescued and forgiven.

Practice confession as a family. Pick one area where sin shows up. Anger. Lying. Disrespect. Greed. Each person names one recent example. Keep names brief. Confess to God in prayer. Then ask forgiveness from each other when sin harmed someone. Joy grows after confession because shame loses power.

Strengthen belief through memory. Post Romans 10:9 in a visible place. Say the verse together once each day. Use the same time. After seven days, each person tries to say the verse without help. Praise effort, not performance.

Let joy lead to witness. Choose one person outside your home. Pray for this person by name. Ask God for an opening to speak about Jesus. When an opening comes, speak one simple sentence. "Jesus saved me, and Jesus leads my life." Offer to pray with the person.

Joy deepens through worship. Sing one song about the cross and resurrection this week. Keep focus on Jesus.

Discussion Questions

1. What does "Jesus is Lord" change in your daily choices?
2. Why does the resurrection matter for your faith?
3. What step will you take this week to confess sin quickly?
4. Who will you pray for and speak to about Jesus?

Family Prayer

Father, thank You for saving us through Jesus. Give us trusting hearts. Give us words to confess Jesus as Lord. Help our home turn from sin and follow Christ. Fill our days with joy rooted in salvation. Amen.

Part 2: Family Life in Christ

Week 11: Serving One Another

"For you have been called to live in freedom, my brothers and sisters. But don't use your freedom to satisfy your sinful nature. Instead, use your freedom to serve one another in love." - Galatians 5:13

God calls your family to serve. Service grows from freedom in Christ. Freedom does not point toward self. Freedom points toward love in action.

Service starts at home. You serve through daily choices. You serve through words and tone. You serve through small actions done without praise. Family life gives many chances to practice service.

Serving one another means you notice needs early. You listen with care. You help without waiting for a reward. You clean without being asked. You share time without complaint. These choices shape character.

Service requires intention. Feelings often resist service. Fatigue blocks service. Pride blocks service. God calls you to act anyway. Obedience comes before comfort.

Teach service with structure. Assign clear responsibilities. Each person owns tasks. Tasks match age and ability. No task stands beneath any person. Parents model service through visible effort. Children learn through example.

Use words that support service. Say thank you for effort. Say well done for follow through. Avoid sarcasm. Avoid comparison. Speak truth with calm.

Correct when service stops. Address the issue early. Speak directly. Set a clear consequence. Follow through. Restore with grace. Pray together after correction.

Link service to love for Christ. Explain purpose. Service honors God. Service builds unity. Service trains the heart. Repeat this truth often.

Choose one service focus for the week. Help at home. Care for a neighbor. Write a note. Prepare a meal. Pray for someone in need. Keep the focus narrow.

End each day with a review. Ask one question. "Where did you serve today?" Each person answers in one sentence. Thank God for growth.

Service shapes family culture. Over time, habits form. Love shows through action. Faith becomes visible.

Discussion Questions

1. Where does service feel hardest at home?
2. What task helps train service this week?
3. How do words support service in your family?
4. What example will parents set this week?

Family Prayer

Father, thank You for freedom through Christ. Teach our family to serve with love. Remove pride and selfishness. Strengthen obedience in daily tasks. Shape our home through faithful service. Amen.

Week 12: Forgiving Freely

"Make allowance for each other's faults, and forgive anyone who offends you. Remember, the Lord forgave you, so you must forgive others." - Colossians 3:13

Forgiveness belongs in family life. Sin hurts people close to you. A sharp tone. A broken promise. A selfish choice. These wounds grow when you hold them.

Colossians 3:13 gives two commands. Make allowance for faults. Forgive offenses. God ties your forgiveness to the Lord's forgiveness toward you. Your forgiveness flows from grace received.

Forgiving freely starts with honesty. Name the offense in plain words. Speak to the person, not about the person. Use one sentence. "You spoke with contempt." "You lied." "You ignored my request." Avoid long speeches.

Own your sin first. Start with your part. Say, "I sinned when I raised my voice." "I sinned when I mocked you." Confession lowers defenses.

Then forgive. Say the words. "I forgive you." Do not add threats. Do not hold the offense as leverage. Release the debt.

Then rebuild trust with action. Forgiveness restores fellowship. Trust rebuilds through consistent behavior. Set one clear repair step. Replace what was damaged. Do the task again. Tell the truth to the person harmed. Apologize to siblings.

Some offenses repeat. Forgiveness remains required. Wise limits remain too. If a child keeps breaking a rule, keep consequences. If hurtful words keep returning, set a pause rule. Step away for five minutes. Return for calm talk. Forgiveness and boundaries work together.

Teach children to forgive early. Use a simple script.

- I was wrong.

- Please forgive me.

- I forgive you.

1. What will you do next time?

Practice with small conflicts. Sibling fights offer daily training. Parents must model forgiveness too. Ask forgiveness from your children when you sin. Children learn sincerity from your tone and follow through.

Make forgiveness a daily habit. Use a bedtime check.

Ask, "Do you need to forgive someone today." Ask, "Do you need to ask forgiveness?" Keep answers brief. Pray for clean hearts. Sleep follows easier when bitterness leaves.

Watch for false forgiveness. False forgiveness uses silence. False forgiveness avoids the person. False forgiveness brings the offense up later in another argument. Choose real forgiveness. Real forgiveness ends scorekeeping.

This week, choose one unresolved offense. Address the person within twenty four hours. Speak the truth. Forgive. Repair.

Discussion Questions

1. What offense lingers in your home?
2. What makes forgiveness hard for you?
3. What repair step restores trust after an apology?
4. What rule will help your family handle repeated offenses?

Family Prayer

Lord, You forgave us through Christ. Train our hearts to forgive. Expose bitterness. Give us humble words. Teach us to confess sin fast. Help our home practice mercy and truth. Amen.

Week 13: Honoring Parents

"Children, obey your parents because you belong to the Lord, for this is the right thing to do. Honor your father and mother. This is the first commandment with a promise: If you honor your father and mother, things will go well for you, and you will have a long life on the earth." - Ephesians 6:1-3

Honor starts with obedience. God speaks to children with clear words. Obey your parents. Honor your father and mother.

Obedience means you do what your parents ask. You do it without delay. You do it without arguing. You do it without eye rolling or mocking.

Honor goes deeper than obedience. Honor shows in your tone. Honor shows in your face. Honor shows in how you talk about your parents when they are not in the room. Honor shows in how you respond when you disagree.

God connects honor with a promise. God calls honor right. God also links honor with good outcomes. You do not obey to control outcomes. You obey because God commands honor.

Obedience answers the question, "Did you do what you were told?" Honor answers the question, "How did you respond while doing it?"

Practice honor in daily moments. When you wake up, greet your parents with respect. When a parent speaks, stop what you are doing and listen. When a parent asks for help, help without complaint. When you disagree, speak with calm words.

Honor also includes care. As children grow, obedience changes. Honor remains. Honor looks like respect, attention, help, gratitude, and honest conversation. Honor does not require agreement with every opinion. Honor requires respect in every interaction.

This week, watch for one warning sign. A fast, sharp tone. A slow, defiant response. A habit of excuses. Address the first sign. Do not wait for a blowup. Correct early. Encourage growth.

Discussion Questions

1. What does obedience look like in your home?
2. What does honor look like in your tone and words?
3. What habit breaks honor most often in your family?
4. What consequence plan will you use for disobedience and disrespect?

Family Prayer

Father, You command honor. Help our children obey with respect. Help our parents lead with clarity and patience. Forgive our disobedience and pride. Train our words and actions. Build a home marked by honor for Your glory. Amen.

Week 14: Speaking with Kindness

"A gentle answer turns away wrath, but a harsh word stirs up anger." - Proverbs 15:1

Words shape family life. Kind words lower tension. Harsh words raise anger. God shows a clear contrast. Tone matters as much as content.

Kind speech begins with awareness. Notice volume. Notice timing. Notice facial expression. Many conflicts grow from tone alone.

Kindness in speech still speaks truth. Boundaries stay firm. Correction stays clear. Kindness guides how words arrive.

Create shared speech rules for everyone.

- Rule one. No yelling. Rule two. No insults. Rule three. No mocking. Rule four. No talking over others.

Post the rules in a common space. Adults follow the same rules. Kids watch closely.

Use a pause when emotions rise. Stop for five seconds. Take one breath. Then speak.

Choose short sentences. Say what needs to be said without extra words. Avoid sarcasm. Avoid labels.

Practice repair after harsh words.

- Step one. Stop the talk. Step two. Name the wrong choice. "I spoke with anger." Step three. Ask forgiveness. Step four. Speak again with kindness.

Make kindness visible each day. Say please. Say thank you. Say sorry. Say I forgive you.

Plan for hard moments. Mornings and bedtimes test patience. Hunger and fatigue add pressure. Slow the pace during these times.

Use one family exercise this week. At one meal, each person shares one moment where kind words helped. Keep sharing brief.

Kind speech protects trust. Kind speech invites honesty. Kind speech reflects obedience to God.

Discussion Questions

1. When do unkind words show up most often?
2. Which rule helps speech stay kind?
3. What phrase helps calm tension?
4. How will everyone repair after harsh words?

Family Prayer

Lord, guide our mouths. Train our family to speak with kindness. Guard tone and timing. Help every person choose gentle words. Amen.

Week 15: Living in Peace

"If it is possible, as far as it depends on you, live at peace with everyone."
- Romans 12:18

Peace starts with your next response. God places responsibility on you. You answer for your words, your tone, and your actions.

Peace in a family does not mean full agreement. Peace means you refuse to turn disagreement into harm.

When conflict starts, slow down first. Notice the first signs. A tight jaw. A fast reply. A raised voice. Take one slow breath. Say a short prayer under your breath. Then speak.

Use simple words. Say what happened. Say what you need. Avoid blame. Avoid mind reading. If you are upset, say so without attacking. If you need time, ask for time.

If you are a child, peace looks like obeying without arguing. Peace looks like telling the truth fast. Peace looks like asking for help instead of yelling.

If you are a parent, peace looks like a calm correction. Peace looks like clear directions. Peace looks like follow through without anger.

If you are a teen, peace looks like respect in disagreement. Peace looks like stepping away before words turn sharp. Peace looks like returning to finish a hard talk with self control.

Peace also requires repair. After a blowup, go back. Do not let distance grow. Name the wrong choice in plain words. Ask forgiveness. Give forgiveness when asked. Then take one step to make things right.

Redo a chore. Replace what was broken. Speak a kind sentence after harsh words. Help the person you hurt.

Pick one daily moment to practice peace. Use dinner, the car ride, or bedtime. Each person shares one small win and one moment that needs repair. Keep sharing short. No lectures. No blaming. Pray together.

Peace grows through repeated choices. When you fail, return fast. Repent fast. Repair fast.

Discussion Questions

1. Where does conflict start most often in your home?
2. What words help you calm down before speaking?
3. What repair step helps your family reconnect after conflict?
4. What choice will you make today to support peace?

Family Prayer

Lord, teach us to live at peace as far as it depends on us. Guard our mouths. Guide our tone. Help us repent fast and forgive fully. Build peace in our home through obedience to You. Amen.

Week 16: Working with Diligence

"Work willingly at whatever you do, as though you were working for the Lord rather than for people." - Colossians 3:23

Diligence means steady effort. You start tasks. You finish tasks. You do not cut corners. God cares about how you work, even in small jobs at home.

This verse speaks to everyone. Parents work. Children work. Teens work. Work includes school, chores, paid jobs, caring for others, and serving in church. God sees each part.

Your reason matters. You work for the Lord. People notice effort, yet people do not set your value. God does. When you remember this truth, you bring care to ordinary duties.

Look at your home first. Diligence shows up in daily routines. Beds made. Dishes washed. Homework done. Shoes put away. Trash taken out. When these tasks slide, stress rises. When you work with care, peace grows.

Start with one clear plan. Each person chooses one daily job. Write jobs on paper. Place paper where everyone sees. Set a simple time. After school. Before dinner. Before screen time. Check work, then redo when needed.

Work willingly means no complaining. Complaining drains the room. Complaining teaches others to resist work. Replace complaints with action. If you feel annoyed, name the feeling to God in prayer, then move your feet.

Work with focus. Put the phone away. Turn off distractions. Set a short timer. Ten minutes of full effort beats an hour of half effort. Younger kids benefit from short bursts. Teens benefit from clear deadlines.

Work with honesty. Do the full job. Wipe the whole counter. Read the whole assignment. Tell the truth about progress. If you forgot, admit your wrong choice fast. Fix the miss. Do not hide.

Work with growth in mind. Skill builds over time. If you struggle with math, practice one problem set each day. If you struggle with a messy room, clear one area each night. If you struggle with time, pack a bag before bed, choose clothes.

Parents, lead through example. Let your children see you do hard tasks without anger. Let them hear you say, "I will finish what I started." When you fail, admit your sin. Then restart with a plan.

Children, diligence honors God and helps your family. When you do your part, you bless others. You also train your future life. A strong habit now serves you later.

Use one family check each evening. Ask two questions. What work did you finish today? What work did you avoid today? Keep answers short. No blaming. Choose one fix for tomorrow. Then thank one person for one specific effort.

Diligence does not mean nonstop work. Rest matters. God designed rest. Diligence means you handle duties before play. You protect sleep. You treat school and work hours with respect. You also leave room for worship and time together.

This week, pick one area where effort stays low. Choose one change. Practice for seven days. Watch what God grows in you.

Discussion Questions

1. Where do you tend to quit early?
2. What distraction pulls you away from work?
3. What daily job will you own this week?
4. How will you remind each other to work for the Lord?

Family Prayer

Lord, guide our hands and minds. Help us work with willing hearts. Forgive lazy habits. Build steady effort in each person. Let our work honor You and bless our home. Amen.

Week 17: Showing Patience

"Understand this, my dear brothers and sisters: You must all be quick to listen, slow to speak, and slow to get angry. Human anger does not produce the righteousness God desires." - James 1:19-20

Patience starts with slowing down. Every family faces moments that test self-control: running late, messy rooms, forgotten chores, or harsh words. God calls you to pause instead of react.

Patience shows up first in how you listen. When someone speaks, look at them. Do not interrupt. Let them finish. Listening gives space for understanding. Anger closes that space.

Next comes your speech. Words come fast when frustration rises. Slow them. If needed, say nothing for a few seconds. Pray quietly before answering. Ask God for calm thoughts and clear words.

Anger feels powerful in the moment but weakens peace. Harsh reactions fix little. They teach fear, not respect. Gentle correction teaches strength and love.

Parents show patience by guiding instead of shouting. Children show patience by accepting direction without rolling eyes or walking away. Teens show patience by holding back quick replies and choosing respect even when they disagree.

Patience is not natural; it grows through practice. When the house feels tense, try this: stop talking, breathe once, then restart the moment with softer words. This simple habit changes how your family handles pressure.

You can build patience through preparation. Tiredness, hunger, and rushing make patience harder. Plan meals, rest, and time buffers. A few minutes of order prevent hours of conflict.

Each evening, talk about one moment when patience worked and one moment when it failed. Keep it short and honest. No blaming. Pray together for more control the next day.

When you lose patience, own it fast. Say, "I was wrong." Do not excuse it. Ask forgiveness. Then try again. Failure can teach more than success when it ends with humility.

Patience grows stronger through prayer, practice, and grace. God stays patient with you every day. Let that truth guide how you treat one another.

Discussion Questions

1. When do you lose patience most easily?
2. What helps you slow down before reacting?
3. How can your family support each other in staying calm?
4. What will you do differently when frustration builds?

Family Prayer

Lord, thank You for Your patience with us. Teach us to slow our words and calm our hearts. Help us listen more, speak less, and choose kindness over anger. Fill our home with peace through patience. Amen.

Week 18: Humility Before God

"So humble yourselves under the mighty power of God, and at the right time he will lift you up in honor." - 1 Peter 5:6

Humility means knowing your place before God. You depend on Him for every breath, every gift, every outcome. Pride wants control. Humility remembers who is in charge.

A humble family gives credit to God first. You thank Him before meals, before sleep, and before new plans. You ask for His help when things feel hard. You give thanks when prayers are answered.

Humility shows in small choices. Listening instead of arguing. Saying thank you instead of complaining. Asking for forgiveness instead of defending yourself. Letting someone else go first. These quiet acts build peace in a home.

Pride grows fast when left alone. You notice it when you refuse help, or when you always want the last word. You notice it when you speak over others or need to prove you are right. God calls you to drop pride and walk in trust.

Parents show humility by admitting mistakes. Children show humility by accepting correction. Teens show humility by taking advice even when it feels uncomfortable. Everyone in the family practices the same truth: God leads, we follow.

Humility does not mean weakness. It means strength under control. A humble person stands firm in truth but does not boast. A humble family honors God through obedience, not noise.

Make this week a practice of lowering yourself before God. Start each morning with one sentence: "Lord, You are God, and I depend on You today." Let that shape how you treat others.

If conflict happens, humble yourself first. Say, "I was wrong." Say it without excuses. Pride protects image; humility restores peace.

Each evening, take one minute to reflect. Where did you show humility today? Where did pride lead your choices? Be honest. Ask God to help you change one thing tomorrow.

Humility brings peace because it removes competition. It replaces blame with service. It reminds everyone that family is not about who wins, but who honors God together.

Discussion Questions

1. When do you notice pride showing up in your words or actions?
2. What does humility look like in your daily choices?
3. How can your family remind each other to stay humble before God?
4. What is one area you need to surrender to God this week?

Family Prayer

Father, teach us to walk humbly with You. Remove pride from our hearts. Help us listen, confess, and obey. Keep us steady under Your power and lift us up at the right time. Amen.

Week 19: Encouraging Each Other

"So encourage each other and build each other up, just as you are already doing."- 1 Thessalonians 5:11

Encouragement strengthens your home. Encouragement speaks hope and truth. Encouragement points a person toward God and next steps.

Encouragement starts with attention. Look for effort. Look for growth. Look for a moment where someone kept going. Then speak.

Use words with names. Say, "Liam, I saw you clean up without being asked." Say, "Mom, thank you for making time for my talk." Say, "Dad, you stayed calm when plans changed." Specific words land.

Encouragement also includes correction with care. When someone fails, speak truth without shame. Say, "You lied, and lying breaks trust." Then add, "Confess, repair, and choose the truth next time." Keep the focus on obedience and repair.

God calls you to build each other up. Building up means you help someone stand firm. You help someone carry a task. You help someone return to God after sin.

Practice encouragement in daily rhythms each day.

Morning words set direction. Before school or work, speak one sentence to each person. Keep sentences short. "God is with you today." "Work with focus." "Tell the truth." "Show respect."

Meal times support connection. At one meal, each person shares one win from the day. Wins stay small. Then each person gives one encouragement to another person at the table. No teasing. No jokes at someone's expense.

Encouragement matters during conflict. Anger pushes harsh words. Choose a different path. Say, "I want peace with you." Say, "You matter to me." Then address the problem with calm words. These sentences lower heat and keep respect in place.

Encouragement also needs listening. When a person shares pain, do not rush to fix it. Ask, "What do you need from me?" Then give support. Pray with the person. Sit close. Offer help with one task.

Children need encouragement with clear structure. Praise effort and obedience. Say, "You obeyed fast." Say, "You finished your homework." Then link encouragement to God. Say, "God loves obedience." This trains the heart.

Teens need encouragement with respect. Notice responsible choices. Notice self control. Notice kindness to siblings. Say, "I trust you with this task." Trust builds maturity.

Parents need encouragement too. Parenting drains energy. Speak gratitude to each other. Name one thing your spouse did well. Say, "Thank you for being steady." Say, "Thank you for serving our family."

Choose one family practice for this week. Create an encouragement list. Place a jar or box in a common space. Each person writes one note each day. One sentence. One name. One specific encouragement. Read notes on the seventh day. Thank God for growth.

Watch your words when tired. Fatigue leads to silence or snapping. Plan one reset. When the home feels tense, pause. Drink water. Take two minutes apart. Return and speak one kind sentence.

Encouragement does not ignore sin. Encouragement helps a person face sin and return to God. Encouragement says, "Repent and keep going."

Discussion Questions
1. Who needs encouragement from you right now?
2. What words help you feel supported at home?
3. What sentence will you speak each morning this week?
4. How will your family handle teasing and sarcasm?

Family Prayer
Lord, train our mouths. Help our family speak words that build up. Show us where others need support. Give us courage to correct with care. Help us point each other toward obedience and hope. Amen.

Week 20: Bearing One Another's Burdens

"Share each other's burdens, and in this way obey the law of Christ." - Galatians 6:2

God calls families to carry weight together. Life brings stress, work, sickness, and mistakes. No one is meant to handle those alone. Burden sharing shows love in action.

This verse gives a simple command. Help each other. It means stepping in before someone asks. It means paying attention. It means doing what love requires even when you feel tired.

Start by noticing. Look for quiet signs. Someone moves slower. Someone grows short in tone. Someone hides in their room. Ask a calm question: "Are you okay?" Then listen. Listening is often the first help.

At home, burden sharing looks practical. Help with chores when another person is overwhelmed. Offer to watch younger siblings. Write a kind note to someone having a hard week. Pray out loud for each other.

Parents carry many hidden burdens. Encourage them with gratitude. Children face pressure too, such as schoolwork, friendships, or expectations. Encourage them with patience. Teens often carry unseen worries. Offer space and time to talk.

Helping does not mean fixing everything. Some burdens stay for a season. You help by walking beside the person, not by taking control.

Keep your words simple. Say, "You are not alone." Say, "I will help." Say, "Let's pray."

Use a family habit this week. Each person shares one thing that feels heavy. Keep it short. No debate. No advice unless asked. After sharing, each person picks one way to support someone else that week. Write it down.

At the end of the week, check in again. Ask, "Did I help?" Ask, "What difference did it make?" Thank God for every small change.

Burden sharing builds humility. It reminds you that strength comes from God, not independence. It teaches compassion, not judgment. It helps a home reflect the love of Christ.

If someone refuses help, stay near in prayer. Keep showing care through steady presence. Do not quit when others grow silent. Love stays patient.

This week, look beyond your home too. Check on a neighbor, classmate, or friend. A short message or small act can lift a spirit weighed down.

Discussion Questions

1. What burden do you carry that you have not shared?
2. What does love look like when someone in your family feels tired?
3. How can you offer help without taking control?
4. Who outside your home could use support this week?

Family Prayer

Lord, teach us to see the needs around us. Give us hearts ready to serve. Help us carry each other's burdens with care and patience. Keep our family united in love and obedience to You. Amen.

Part 3: Growing in Character

Week 21: Honesty Matters

"The Lord detests lying lips, but he delights in those who tell the truth." - Proverbs 12:22

Honesty builds trust. A family built on truth stands strong. Lies, even small ones, break peace and bring distance. God cares deeply about honesty because truth reflects His character.

Honesty starts inside the heart. You decide before you speak whether your words will match reality. Lies come from fear: fear of trouble, fear of shame, or fear of losing control. Truth comes from trust in God. You tell the truth because you answer to Him first.

In family life, honesty shows up every day. When someone asks a question, give the full answer, not part of it. When you break something, admit it. When you forget a task, say so. These small moments shape your reputation and your conscience.

Parents teach honesty by how they respond to truth. If a child confesses a mistake, listen first. Thank them for telling the truth before addressing the problem. Harsh reactions teach hiding. Calm correction builds trust.

Children learn honesty through consistency. Keep promises. Follow through on what you say. Admit when you are wrong. Adults model truth when they apologize and when they resist excuses.

Honesty also means telling the truth with kindness. You can speak the truth and still use a gentle tone. Avoid words that embarrass or shame. Speak correction in private when possible. Truth given in love brings growth.

This week, watch for half-truths and small excuses. They grow into habits. When you catch one, stop right away. Say, "That wasn't the full truth." Then correct it. The goal is not punishment; it's growth in character.

Build an honesty routine in your home. Each night, ask one question: "Was I truthful today?" Each person answers with one sentence. If someone needs to confess, do it simply, then pray for forgiveness together.

Honesty does not promise comfort, but it brings freedom. Lies trap you in guilt and fear. Truth gives peace and clean conscience. God delights in those who choose honesty, even when it costs something.

Discussion Questions

1. When is it hardest for you to tell the truth?
2. How should our family respond when someone confesses?
3. What small habit can help you stay honest?
4. How does honesty build trust at home?

Family Prayer

Lord, help us walk in truth. Give us courage to speak honestly, even when it is hard. Teach us to listen with grace when others confess. Let our family be known for honesty that honors You. Amen.

Week 22: Wisdom from Above

"But the wisdom from above is first pure. It is also peace loving, gentle, and willing to yield to others. It is full of mercy and the fruit of good deeds. It shows no favoritism and is always sincere." - James 3:17

You face choices every day. Some choices feel small. Some choices shape your family for years. You need wisdom, not impulse. You need wisdom from God.

This verse gives a clear test. When you wonder what to do, compare your plan to these words.

First, wisdom from above is pure. Ask yourself if your choice is clean before God. Is there dishonesty? Is there a secret sin? Is there a motive you would hide? Purity means you refuse compromise.

Next, wisdom is peace loving. Peace loving does not mean avoiding truth. Peace loving means you refuse to stir conflict for pride. You do not enjoy winning arguments. You do not speak to hurt.

Wisdom is gentle. Gentleness shows in tone and timing. You correct without crushing. You lead without intimidation. Gentleness protects trust, especially with children.

Wisdom is willing to yield to others. This does not mean you surrender the truth. It means you listen. It means you admit when someone else has a better idea. It means you change direction when you are wrong. In a family, yielding often looks like letting someone else choose, letting someone finish speaking, or letting a plan shift without anger.

Wisdom is full of mercy. Mercy means you do not treat people as they deserve. You choose forgiveness. You choose patience. You remember your own need for grace.

Wisdom produces good deeds. Good deeds are visible. They do not talk only. They show in chores done without being asked. They show in help given to a sibling. They show a parent who serves without resentment.

Wisdom shows no favoritism. In a family, favoritism destroys unity. You do not treat one child as the golden child and another as the problem child. You correct fairly. You praise fairly. You give time with care.

Wisdom is sincere. Sincere words match real intent. Sincere apologies own wrong without excuses. Sincere encouragement speaks truth, not flattery.

When you lack wisdom, ask God for it in prayer. Do not wait until you explode. Pray early. Pray in the car. Pray in the kitchen. God gives direction through His Word and through humble counsel.

Wisdom from above changes a home. It changes how you speak. It changes how you decide. It shapes character in every person.

Discussion Questions

1. What choice do you need wisdom for right now?
2. Which part of James 3:17 challenges you most?
3. Where do you need to be more gentle at home?
4. Where do you need to yield to others this week?

Family Prayer

Father, give our family wisdom from above. Keep our hearts pure. Make our choices peace loving and sincere. Train our words to be gentle. Fill us with mercy and good deeds. Guard us from favoritism. Lead us in Your ways. Amen.

Week 23: The Fruit of the Spirit

"But the Holy Spirit produces this kind of fruit in our lives: love, joy, peace, patience, kindness, goodness, faithfulness, gentleness, and self-control. There is no law against these things." - Galatians 5:22-23

You want a home where faith shows up in daily life. God does not leave you guessing. He names the kind of life the Spirit grows in you. These traits are fruit. Fruit grows over time. Fruit grows from a living root.

You do not grow this fruit by forcing it. You grow it by staying close to Christ. You grow it by choosing obedience when you feel pressure. You grow it by asking the Spirit to lead your words and actions.

Start with love. Love puts people first. Love serves without keeping score. Love speaks truth without cruelty. Ask yourself today, "What loving action will I take in this house."

Joy is more than a good mood. Joy is a settled gladness in God. Joy shows up when you thank God for what is true, even on a hard day. Practice one joy habit. Name one gift from God at dinner.

Peace shows in how you handle stress. Peace shows in a steady tone. Peace shows in quick repair after conflict. If you feel your peace slipping, stop and pray one sentence.

Patience slows your reactions. Patience waits without snapping. Patience stays calm during delays. If you are a parent, patience shapes discipline. If you are a child, patience shapes obedience.

Kindness shows in small words and small help. Kindness says please and thank you. Kindness shares. Kindness checks on a sibling.

Goodness means you choose what is right. Goodness refuses lies and shortcuts. Goodness admits wrong and makes repairs.

Faithfulness means you keep your word. Faithfulness shows up in chores finished, homework done, and promises kept. Faithfulness builds trust.

Gentleness means strength under control. Gentleness corrects without crushing. Gentleness listens before speaking. Gentleness protects the weak.

Self-control means you govern your desires. Self-control holds back harsh words. Self-control limits screens. Self-control says no to sin.

Make this practical as a family this week. Choose one fruit each day. Write the word on a paper. Place it where you see it. In the morning, each person names one action connected to the fruit. At night, each person shares one win and one fail. Keep it short. No blaming.

When you fail, do not hide. Confess fast. Ask forgiveness. Forgive fast. Then try again. Fruit grows through repeated choices.

Ask the Spirit for help. You need God to change what is inside you. You need God to shape your home.

Use a simple check during the day. Before you speak, ask, "Does this show love and self-control?" Before you discipline, ask, "Am I being gentle." Before you choose entertainment, ask, "Will this feed peace." These questions keep the Spirit's fruit in view for your whole family.

Discussion Questions

1. Which fruit is hardest for you right now?
2. What fruit would help your family most this week?
3. What is one action you will take tomorrow to practice that fruit?
4. How will you respond when you fail?

Family Prayer

Holy Spirit, grow Your fruit in our family. Train our hearts toward love. Fill our mouths with kindness. Give us patience and self-control. Help us choose what is good and true. Make our home faithful and gentle. Lead us in peace and joy. Amen.

Week 24: Integrity in Small Things

"If you are faithful in little things, you will be faithful in large ones. But if you are dishonest in little things, you won't be honest with greater responsibilities." - Luke 16:10

Integrity means your actions match God's truth. You do what is right when no one is watching. You keep your word in small moments. You tell the truth even when a lie looks easier. God sees all.

Jesus links small choices to bigger trust. A hidden shortcut trains your heart. A quiet act of honesty trains your heart too. Over time, your family becomes known for trust or known for excuses.

Start with the small places where integrity often slips.

Money. If you find extra change at a store, return it. If you borrow, repay on time. If you owe an apology, speak soon. Teach children to handle money with clean hands.

Work. Do the full chore, not half. Put items where they belong. Finish homework with care. If you rush and miss steps, own the mistake and redo the work.

Words. Say what you mean. Do not promise help, then disappear. If you said yes, follow through. If plans must change, speak early and speak plainly.

Screens. Integrity includes private choices. Keep devices in open spaces. Use agreed limits. If a child breaks a rule, confess without delay.

If a parent breaks a rule, confess without delay. Your home needs one standard.

Truth grows when your home stays safe for confession. When someone tells the truth, respond with calm. Thank the person for honesty, then address the wrong choice. Harsh reactions teach hiding. Calm correction builds trust.

Use a simple family practice for seven days.

Each evening, ask two questions:

Where did I keep my word today?

Where did I cut a corner today?

Each person answers with one sentence. No stories. No blaming. Parents answer first. After answers, choose one repair step. Return an item. Redo a task. Replace what was damaged. Ask forgiveness. Then pray.

Integrity also shapes how you talk about others. Do not spread private information. Do not mock. Do not twist stories to look better. Speak truth with respect.

Watch for common excuses. "I forgot." "I did not hear you." "I thought you meant later." Sometimes these words are true. Sometimes these words hide refusal. Ask one follow up. "What will you do next time?" Then set a plan.

For younger children, keep integrity lessons concrete. Give one job. Check work together. Praise honest confession. Apply a clear consequence for lying. Then restore closeness.

For teens, connect integrity to freedom. More trust brings more responsibility. Less trust brings tighter limits. Speak with respect. Ask for honest reports. Verify when needed, without sarcasm.

For parents, integrity starts with confession. When you lose patience, admit sin. When you break a promise, repair. Children learn integrity through your choices more than your talks.

Integrity in small things prepares your family for bigger tests. Today's tiny choices shape tomorrow's strength.

Discussion Questions

1. Where do small shortcuts show up in our home?
2. What makes honesty hard for you?
3. What repair step feels hardest for you?

4.   What habit will help your family keep integrity this week?

Family Prayer

Father, train our hearts to love truth. Help us keep our word. Expose hidden sin. Give us courage to confess fast and repair fully. Build trust in our home through integrity. Amen.

Week 25: Guarding Your Heart

"Guard your heart above all else, for it determines the course of your life." - Proverbs 4:23

Your heart is your inner life. Your thoughts, desires, and choices flow from it. God tells you to guard it. Not after damage happens. Before.

What you allow in shapes what comes out. If you feed your heart with anger, you will speak with anger. If you feed your heart with envy, you will resent others. If you feed your heart with lust, you will treat people as objects. If you feed your heart with God's Word, you will grow in faith and steadiness.

Guarding your heart starts with attention. Notice what pulls you. Notice what triggers you. Notice what you return to when you feel stressed. Do not ignore patterns.

Guarding your heart includes what you watch and listen to. Music, videos, games, and online content teach values. They train your reactions. They shape what you think is normal. Choose with care.

Make family standards for media. Keep screens in shared spaces. Set time limits. Protect bedtimes. Check what your children watch. Check what you watch. Adults do not get a separate standard.

Guarding your heart includes friendships. Friends shape your choices. Good friends encourage obedience. Bad friends pull you toward sin. Teach your children to choose friends who respect God's ways. Teach them to leave conversations that mock what is right.

Guarding your heart includes your own words. Complaining feeds bitterness. Gossip feeds pride. Crude speech feeds impurity. Change inputs by changing speech. When you catch yourself, stop and replace the words.

Guarding your heart includes what you think about in private. Some thoughts land without invitation. You choose whether they stay. Replace sinful thoughts with truth. Use short Scripture statements. Use prayer. Use a change of activity. Do not sit and feed temptation.

Teach this to your children with simple steps.

Step one. Notice what you are feeling.

Step two. Name it to God.

Step three. Choose the right response.

Help them learn triggers. Hunger, tiredness, jealousy, and fear lead to poor choices. Prepare ahead with food, rest, and clear routines.

Choose one family practice this week. Do a heart check at dinner.

Each person answers two questions: What did I let into my heart today? What came out of my heart today?

Keep answers short. No blaming. If a person shares something heavy, respond with calm. Pray together. If you need change, choose one clear step for tomorrow.

Guarding your heart also means filling it with what is true. Read Scripture daily. Pray daily. Worship weekly. Speak gratitude in the home. These habits build protection.

When you fail, do not hide. Confess to God. Ask forgiveness from people you hurt. Remove what led you into sin. Then replace it with a better habit.

Your heart sets direction. Guard it with God's help. Your family will feel the results.

Discussion Questions

1. What input affects your heart most?
2. What habit do you need to change this week?
3. What standard will protect your home from harmful content?
4. How will you replace a wrong pattern with a right one?

Family Prayer

Lord, help us guard our hearts. Show us what harms our inner life. Give us strength to remove sinful inputs. Fill our home with Your Word and truth. Lead our choices so our lives honor You. Amen.

Week 26: Contentment in Every Season

"For I have learned how to be content with whatever I have." - Philippians 4:11

Contentment is learned. It does not appear on its own. Your heart wants more, or different, or easier. God trains you to rest in what He provides.

Paul wrote these words while facing hardship. He did not base contentment on comfort. He learned to trust God in every situation. This week, you practice the same trust as a family.

Contentment starts with honest talk. Name where you feel discontent. Money. Time. Space. Work. School. Friendships. Health. Then bring those needs to God without complaining.

Complaining spreads fast in a home. One negative comment becomes a habit. Contentment breaks that habit. Contentment says, "God has provided, and we will be thankful and faithful."

Contentment does not mean you stop working. It means you stop grumbling. You still plan. You still save. You still study. You still improve skills. You do it with gratitude instead of resentment.

Teach children the difference between needs and wants. Needs include food, clothing, shelter, safety, and care. Wants include extra treats, new devices, and status items. When a want feels urgent, pause and speak truth. "We have what we need today." Then redirect the heart.

Practice gratitude as a family. Each day, each person names three gifts from God. Keep gifts specific. A meal. A friend. A safe ride. A kind teacher. A clean bed. Gratitude trains contentment.

Limit comparison. Comparison steals peace. Social media often fuels comparison. If comparison rises, name it. "I am comparing." Then stop feeding it. Put the phone away. Focus on what God gave your home.

Contentment also shapes how you handle disappointments. When plans change, you can explode or you can adjust. When someone else gets what you wanted, you can envy or you can bless. These choices show what rules your heart.

Use one simple practice this week. Choose one "contentment sentence" for your family. Say it when you feel discontent.

- "God is good to us today." "We will be thankful and faithful." "We have enough for today."

Pick one and use it for seven days.

Add a contentment habit to your spending. Before buying something new, wait one day. During that day, pray about the purchase. Ask if it is needed. Ask if it fits your budget. Ask if it will feed gratitude or feed pride.

Contentment also includes generosity. Giving breaks greed. Choose one act of giving this week. Share food. Give clothes. Serve someone in need. Help a neighbor. When you give, your heart learns to rest.

When you fail, confess quickly. Ask God to forgive grumbling. Ask family members to forgive harsh words. Then restart with gratitude.

Contentment is a steady trust in God's care. Your season will change. God stays faithful.

Discussion Questions

1. Where do you feel discontent most often?
2. What triggers complaining in your home?
3. What gratitude habit will you practice this week?
4. How will you limit comparison in your family?

Family Prayer

Father, teach us contentment. Forgive our grumbling and envy. Help us trust Your care in every season. Train our home to be thankful, faithful, and generous. Amen.

Week 27: Faith in Action

"Faith by itself, if it is not accompanied by action, is dead." - James 2:17

Faith is more than words. Faith shows through choices. Your family learns what you trust by watching what you do.

James speaks with clarity. Faith without action is dead. Dead faith agrees with truth, then stays still. Living faith moves toward obedience.

Start here. When you trust God, you obey God. Obedience looks plain. You forgive after hurt. You tell the truth when a lie feels safer. You serve when energy runs low. You pray when worry rises.

Action does not earn salvation. Jesus saves by grace. Action proves where your trust rests. Parents lead. Children practice. Teens grow by taking responsibility.

Pick one area in your home where faith needs movement.

Begin with words. If you follow Jesus, your speech must match His ways. Speak with respect. Refuse insults. Stop gossip. Admit wrong fast. Make repairs with clear steps.

Next, look at work. Chores and school are training grounds. Finish tasks. Do your best. Put items back. Keep promises. When you fail, confess, then redo the work.

Next, look at money and possessions. Faith acts through giving. Set aside a small amount. Give the gift to church or to a need you know. Let children help choose the gift. Talk about reasons for giving. Giving trains trust.

Next, look at time. Faith acts through priorities. Choose a daily time for Scripture and prayer. Keep the time short and steady. Protect the time from distractions. Let your children see you show up.

Faith acts through mercy. When someone fails, do not crush the person. Correct with truth. Then help the person stand up and try again. Mercy is action.

Faith acts outside your home. Look for one person who needs help this week. A neighbor. A classmate. A relative. Choose one act of support. A meal. A ride. A message. A visit. Then follow through.

Keep actions small. Big promises often break. Small actions build habits. Choose one verse from family reading. Ask, "What command appears here?" Then do one part of the command before bedtime. Record results on paper. Thank God for growth.

Use a family plan for seven days.

Read James 2:17 out loud once a day.

Choose one faith action for your home. Examples are a shared chore list, a screen limit, or a daily prayer time.

Choose one faith action for someone outside your home.

At dinner, each person shares one action from the day. One sentence is enough.

When you fall short, do not pretend. Say, "I did not follow through." Then choose a new step for tomorrow. God trains you through practice, repentance, and steady effort.

Faith in action changes a home. Trust grows. Unity grows. Children learn obedience in real moments, not theory. Your family becomes quick to repent, quick to serve, and quick to forgive.

Discussion Questions

1. Where does your faith show most clearly at home?
2. Where do your actions fail to match your words?
3. What one action will you take today to obey Jesus?
4. Who outside your home needs practical help from your family this week?

Family Prayer

Lord Jesus, grow living faith in our family. Show us one step of obedience for today. Help us follow through with action. Forgive lazy habits and empty words. Teach our home to serve, give, repent, and forgive with steady hearts. Amen.

Week 28: Compassion for Others

"Instead, be kind to each other, tenderhearted, forgiving one another, just as God through Christ has forgiven you." - Ephesians 4:32

Compassion means you notice pain and respond with care. Compassion is not a feeling you keep inside. Compassion moves you toward action.

God gives three clear directions in this verse. Be kind. Be tenderhearted. Forgive. These choices shape how your family treats each other and how your family treats people outside your home.

Kindness shows in small words and small help. You hold a door. You share. You speak with respect. You offer to carry something heavy. You check on a sibling who looks upset. Kindness costs little, yet it changes the room.

Tenderhearted means your heart stays soft. A hard heart mocks weakness. A soft heart takes people seriously. A soft heart listens. A soft heart does not rush to blame.

Tenderheartedness starts with listening. When someone shares, you stop other tasks. You look at the person. You let the person finish. Then you ask, "What do you need from me?" Some people need help. Some people need prayer. Some people need quiet support.

Forgiveness belongs to compassion. When someone hurts you, you can hold the offense or you can release it. God ties your forgiveness to Christ. You forgive because you have been forgiven.

Compassion also includes truth. If someone sins, you do not ignore it. You respond with correction that protects the person. You speak in a calm tone. You keep the focus on the behavior. You guide toward repentance and repair.

Practice compassion at home first. Family life gives daily chances.

When someone is sick, offer help without being asked.

When someone fails, speak encouragement and give a path forward.

When someone is sad, sit with the person and pray.

When someone is angry, stay calm and ask what is wrong.

Teach children to notice others. Ask simple questions at dinner.

Who looked lonely today? Who needed help today? Who did you encourage today?

Then choose one action for tomorrow.

Compassion grows when you limit selfish habits. Selfishness keeps eyes on self. Compassion lifts eyes to others. Train your family to look outward.

Choose one compassion practice for this week.

Pick one person outside your home who needs support. It can be a neighbor, teacher, church member, or friend. Do one act of kindness. Write a note. Bring food. Offer help with a task. Pray for the person by name.

Also practice compassion inside the home. Each person chooses one family member to serve for the week. Keep the action simple and quiet. A cleaned space. A kind message. A shared chore. A prayer spoken out loud.

At the end of the week, talk about what you learned. Compassion changes you too. It grows patience. It builds unity. It reflects Christ.

Discussion Questions

1. When is it hardest for you to show compassion?
2. What helps you keep your heart soft?
3. Who in your family needs extra kindness right now?
4. Who outside your home will you help this week?

Family Prayer

Father, make our family kind and tenderhearted. Help us forgive as we have been forgiven in Christ. Open our eyes to people in need. Give us courage to act with compassion and truth. Amen.

Week 29: Self-Control in All Things

"All athletes are disciplined in their training. They do it to win a prize that will fade away, but we do it for an eternal prize." - 1 Corinthians 9:25

Self-control means you choose what is right, even when you want something else. You control words, habits, and reactions. You do not let cravings lead. You let God's commands lead.

Paul uses athletes as an example. Athletes train with discipline because they want a prize. Their prize fades. Your prize lasts. God calls you to train your life with purpose.

Self-control touches every part of family life.

Self-control in speech means you stop harsh words. You do not interrupt. You do not insult. You do not explode. If you feel anger rising, you pause and breathe, then speak with restraint.

Self-control in time means you do what you must do before what you want to do. Homework before screens. Chores before games. Sleep before late scrolling.

Self-control in food means you eat with gratitude, not greed. You stop when you have enough. You do not hide food or sneak treats.

Self-control in money means you do not buy to feel better. You plan. You save. You give. You avoid impulse spending.

Self-control in entertainment means you choose what is clean. You turn off what feeds sin. You avoid content that trains lust, violence, or disrespect.

Self-control also includes your body. You choose rest. You choose movement. You avoid habits that damage health.

Self-control grows through training. Training starts small.

Pick one area where your family struggles most. Choose one clear change for seven days. Keep it simple. Write it down.

Examples.

- No screens during meals. Devices stay out of bedrooms. One hour of homework before games. Use calm voices during disagreement. No snacks after a set time at night.

Then practice daily.

Make a plan for hard moments. When temptation hits, use a quick response.

- Stop. Pray one sentence. Choose the next right action.

This works for anger, cravings, and distraction.

Parents model training. Children learn what self-control looks like by watching adults handle stress. If you blow up, confess fast. If you break a rule, own it. Restart with humility.

Children and teens also train. If you lose control, you repair. You ask forgiveness. You replace harm with one good action. Then you try again.

Self-control does not mean perfection. It means steady direction. Over time, habits change. Your home becomes calmer. Your work improves. Your trust grows.

End each day with a short check.

Where did I show self-control today? Where did I give in today?

Keep answers short. No blaming. Pray together.

You train for an eternal prize. That prize is life with Christ. Let self-control shape your daily choices.

Discussion Questions

1. Where do you struggle most with self-control?
2. What temptation hits you most often?
3. What rule will help your family train this week?
4. What will you do when you fail?

Family Prayer

Lord, train our hearts and habits. Help us choose what is right when temptation comes. Give us discipline in speech, time, and desires. Forgive failures and strengthen obedience. Keep our eyes on the eternal prize. Amen.

Week 30: Courage to Stand Firm

"Be on guard. Stand firm in the faith. Be courageous. Be strong." - 1 Corinthians 16:13

Courage shows up when you face pressure and still obey God. Standing firm means you do not bend when wrong feels normal. Your family needs this strength.

Paul gives four commands. Be on guard. Stand firm. Be courageous. Be strong. These words are for adults, teens, and children.

Being on guard means you pay attention. You notice what pulls your heart away from Christ. You notice habits that weaken your home. Talk about dangers as a family. Name them. Screens. crude jokes. cheating at school. gossip. anger. hiding. When you name a threat, you are ready to resist.

Stand firm in the faith means you hold to what God has said. You do not change the truth to fit friends. You do not hide faith to avoid laughter. Standing firm starts with Scripture. Read it. Learn it. Speak it.

Being courageous means you act even when you feel fear. Courage is not loud. Courage is obedience in a hard moment. A child shows courage by telling the truth after a mistake. A teen shows courage by walking away from a group that mocks what is right. A parent shows courage by setting limits with love and holding them.

Being strong means you lean on God, not on pride. Strength grows through prayer, rest, wise routines, and steady repentance. When you are tired, temptation hits harder. Stay close to God and close to your family.

Practice courage in small ways. Small stands prepare you for bigger stands. Choose honesty in small things. Choose kindness when others push you to be cruel. Choose worship when other plans compete. Choosing forgiveness when holding a grudge feels easier.

Make one courage plan for this week. Each person names one place where pressure hits. School. work. friends. media. Each person chooses one firm response. Keep responses simple. "I will not lie." "I will not join in mocking." "I will stop a show that feeds sin." "I will speak with respect when I am upset." Write the responses down. Check in each day for one minute.

Role play hard moments. Practice saying no with a voice. Practice leaving a room. Practice calling a parent. Practice praying. Training before pressure makes obedience simpler when the moment arrives.

When someone fails, do not shame. Bring the person back to truth. Confess. Ask forgiveness. Make one repair. Then stand again. Courage grows through return, not through hiding.

Teach your family a short sentence for pressure. "I belong to Jesus." Say it out loud at home. Children remember short phrases. Teens need them too.

Courage also means you protect others. If a sibling is picked on, step in with calm words. If a friend asks you to sin, say no and walk away.

God calls you to stand firm today. Start with the next choice. God will help you stay faithful.

Discussion Questions

1. Where do you feel pressure to compromise?
2. What helps you stay on guard?
3. What is one firm response you will practice this week?
4. How will our family help each other stand again after failure?

Family Prayer

Lord, keep us on guard. Help us stand firm in faith. Give us courage to obey when fear rises. Make us strong through Your Word and prayer. Help our home honor Jesus in public and in private. Amen.

Part 4: Living Out the Gospel

Week 31: Sharing Your Faith

"Go therefore and make disciples of all nations, baptizing them in the name of the Father and of the Son and of the Holy Spirit, teaching them to observe all that I have commanded you." – Matthew 28:19-20

Jesus gave this command before returning to heaven. He spoke to His followers and gave them a job. That job still applies to every believer today. Your family has a role in sharing the message of Jesus. You do not need a stage. You need faith and obedience.

This verse gives four actions. Go. Make disciples. Baptize. Teach. Start with go. Go means you move toward people. At school. At work. At practice. In your neighborhood. You do not wait for perfect conditions. You look around and say, "Who needs to hear about Jesus?"

Next is to make disciples. A disciple is someone who learns and follows. You do not force anyone. You invite. You share truth. You answer questions. You stay kind when rejected. You stay clear when others confuse the message. A disciple learns from Jesus and lives like Jesus.

Baptism comes after belief. It shows that a person now belongs to Christ. In your home, talk openly about baptism. If a child wants to follow Jesus, explain that baptism is a public step of obedience. Keep it clear. Baptism does not save. Jesus saves. Baptism shows what Jesus already did.

Teaching comes next. When someone believes in Jesus, the work is not over. You help them grow. You show them how to read the Bible. You pray with them. You point them back to Scripture when life feels hard. You stay faithful even when results take time.

Evangelism starts in the home. Your children hear the gospel from you. Parents must speak clearly about sin, salvation, and surrender. Do not assume children know. Ask questions. Use Scripture. Invite response.

You also train your children to speak about Jesus to others. Use short sentences. "Jesus forgave me." "Jesus changed how I treat people." "I trust Jesus when I'm scared." These truths matter. They plant seeds.

As a family, make a plan this week. Choose one person outside your home. Pray for them by name every day. Write their name on paper. Ask God to give you one opportunity to speak about Jesus. If the door opens, speak with calm. Share one thing Jesus has done for you. Then listen. Do not argue. Speak truth and love.

Practice at home. Have each person say one sentence about Jesus. Use clear, personal language. If a child believes but has not been baptized, start the conversation. If someone has doubts, listen and return to Scripture.

You do not need to be perfect. You need to be available. God works through small steps. One word. One verse. One act of kindness. These things open hearts.

Obedience to the Great Commission starts with your next conversation. Make that conversation count.

Discussion Questions

1. What makes you nervous about sharing your faith?
2. Who in your life needs to hear about Jesus?
3. How can your family pray for boldness this week?
4. What step can you take to explain the gospel clearly?

Family Prayer

Lord Jesus, You gave us a mission. Help us obey. Give us courage to speak Your name. Help us tell others about what You have done. Show us who needs to hear the truth. Make our home a place where the gospel is clear. Use us to help others follow You. Amen.

Week 32: Loving Your Neighbor

"The second is this: 'Love your neighbor as yourself.' There is no commandment greater than these.." – Mark 12:31

Jesus gave two commands that sum up the whole law. Love God. Love your neighbor. This verse covers the second. It is simple to say and hard to live. Families must practice this command daily.

Loving your neighbor starts at home. You speak with respect. You help without being asked. You listen instead of mocking. You choose peace when conflict rises. If love does not show up in your house, it will not show up outside of it.

Your neighbor includes anyone near you. Friends. Classmates. Teachers. People at church. People who frustrate you. People who ignore you. This love is not based on how others treat you. It is based on obedience to God.

Jesus says to love your neighbor as yourself. That means you care about their needs the way you care about your own. You want others to feel safe, respected, and helped. You think about their feelings, not just your own. You treat them how you would want to be treated.

Love also corrects. When a person is wrong, love speaks truth. Not with harshness. Not with pride. Love says, "That path leads to trouble." Love says, "Come back." Love does not ignore sin. Love calls people toward what is good.

This week, focus your home on action. Start with one question: "What does love look like right now?" Ask it before responding. Ask it before making a plan. Let it guide your tone and your timing.

Choose one neighbor to bless. Keep it simple. Bring food. Offer help. Write a note. Invite someone to church. Pray with someone who is hurting. Do not wait for a perfect moment. Love acts.

In your home, make one list. Each person writes one way they want to be treated. Then ask, "How can we give these same things to others?" Use the answers to create a family love plan. Pick one to practice each day.

Love in conflict means you choose calm when others yell. You choose kindness when others mock. You step back instead of pushing forward. You walk away from gossip. You speak peace when others stir trouble. These choices cost you. That is why they show real love.

Talk often about what love is not. Love is not control. Love is not fear. Love is not pressure. Love does not ignore wrong. Love does not quit when things get hard. Jesus did not quit loving. Your family must not either.

When your family fails, restart. Say sorry. Ask forgiveness. Name what went wrong. Make one step to fix it. Love stays close when things feel hard. That is how others will know you follow Jesus.

Discussion Questions

1. What does it mean to love others as yourself?
2. Who do you find hard to love right now?
3. What action will your family take this week to show love?
4. How do you want others to treat you, and how can you give that to them?

Family Prayer

Father, teach us to love like You. Show us how to treat others with kindness and truth. Help us serve without selfishness. Help us forgive when we feel hurt. Let our home be a place where love leads. In Jesus' name. Amen.

Week 33: Caring for the Poor

"Whoever is generous to the poor lends to the Lord, and he will repay him for his deed." – Proverbs 19:17

God cares deeply about the poor. He sees them. He defends them. He provides for them through His people. When your family cares for the poor, you reflect God's heart. You live out your faith through action.

This verse is strong. When you give to the poor, you are giving to God. That means how you treat the poor shows what you believe about God. If you ignore their needs, you ignore the one who made them. If you act with kindness and help, God sees and rewards.

Caring for the poor begins with awareness. Children need to understand that not everyone has what they have. Some people do not have clean clothes, enough food, or a safe place to sleep. Some people feel forgotten. Talk about these things as a family. Use clear, honest words. Avoid pity. Focus on dignity and responsibility.

Teach that generosity is not about amount. It is about the heart. A small gift given with care honors God. A large gift given with pride does not. God sees motive. He values faithfulness. Your job is not to fix every problem. Your job is to respond in love and obedience.

Giving also includes time and effort. You care for the poor when you listen, when you serve, and when you include. You care when you share your lunch with someone at school. You care when you serve meals, donate clothes, or visit someone in need. Each act matters.

Make a plan this week. Choose one way to serve together. Pack food for a shelter. Deliver groceries to a family in need. Set aside part of your allowance or income and give it to a trustworthy ministry. Write one note of encouragement. Make sure your children help decide and participate.

Also check your attitude. Do not speak with pride. Do not act like you are better. Generosity should not make others feel small. Teach your family to serve with respect, not pity. God values every person the same. Your love should reflect that.

Talk about why you give. Explain that everything you have comes from God. Giving is a way to say thank you. Giving is a way to say, "We trust You to keep providing." Giving also keeps your heart from becoming selfish. It trains your home to be open-handed.

Keep one record this week. Write down every act of generosity your family does. Keep it quiet. Do not post about it. Do not seek praise. At the end of the week, thank God for letting you join His work. Ask Him to keep your heart tender toward those in need.

Discussion Questions

1. What does this verse teach us about how God sees the poor?
2. What keeps people from giving or helping?
3. What is one small act of generosity your family will do this week?
4. How can you help others with respect and love, not pride?

Family Prayer

Father, You see every person in need. Help us open our hands and hearts. Remind us that everything we have belongs to You. Teach us to give with joy and to serve with respect. Let our family reflect Your love through our actions. In Jesus' name. Amen.

Week 34: Being the Light

"You are the light of the world. A city set on a hill cannot be hidden." - Matthew 5:14

Jesus gives His people a clear identity. You are the light. Light stands out. Light helps others see. Light brings safety and direction. In a dark world, believers must not blend in. Your family is called to live in a way that points others to God.

This verse is not a suggestion. It is a fact. If you belong to Jesus, you carry His light. The question is not, "Do we shine?" The question is, "Are we hiding it?" Jesus says a city on a hill cannot be hidden. Your words, choices, and attitudes should be clear. People should see something different in your home.

Light comes from God, not from you. You do not produce light. You reflect it. When you stay close to Jesus, His light shows through you. That means the more your family follows Him, the brighter your home will shine.

Start by checking your patterns. Do your neighbors see peace in your family? Do your classmates see kindness in your words? Does your home speak about Jesus with joy and boldness? Light does not whisper. Light does not hide.

Being the light includes your actions in normal life. When you forgive, you shine. When you tell the truth, you shine. When you give, help, or speak with calm in hard moments, you shine. These moments build your family's witness.

This week, choose one public action that reflects Christ. Keep it simple. Bring food to someone. Invite a family to church. Send a message of encouragement. Offer to pray for someone. Do not hide your faith. Speak the name of Jesus.

In your home, talk about light and dark. Name actions that bring light. Name choices that bring darkness. Be specific. Sarcasm in conflict hides the light. Gossip hides the light. Quiet repentance brings the light back.

Children can live as light in school. By including someone who feels left out. By doing what's right when no one watches. By using kind words when others mock. Teens can live as light in hard conversations and in honest decisions.

Teach your children this sentence: "Our home will reflect Jesus today." Write it down. Say it each morning. Let it shape your routines and responses.

At night, ask one question: "How did our family shine the light today?" Keep answers short. Name the actions. Celebrate obedience. Plan for tomorrow.

When you fail, return fast. Ask forgiveness. Correct the wrong. Take the next step. God's mercy restores and strengthens.

The world is watching. Not for perfection, but for truth. Let your home be a steady light in an unsteady world.

Discussion Questions

1. What does it mean to be the light of the world?
2. Where are you tempted to hide your faith?
3. What small action this week can help your family shine?
4. How can you speak the name of Jesus in daily life?

Family Prayer

Lord, thank You for making us light in this world. Help us shine clearly. Keep us from hiding. Give us boldness to speak and live with truth and love. Let others see You through our family. In Jesus' name. Amen.

Week 35: Serving with Joy

"Each of you should use whatever gift you have received to serve others, as faithful stewards of God's grace in its various forms." – 1 Peter 4:10

God gives gifts for a reason. Not for display. Not for pride. Not for control. He gives gifts so you can serve others. Your family has a part in His work. You are stewards, not owners. A steward takes care of something on behalf of the giver.

This verse makes two things clear. Every believer has received a gift. Every believer is called to use it. No one is left out. No one is excused. Serving others is part of following Jesus.

Start with your own home. Children learn to serve by watching how their parents serve. They learn to help by being given real tasks. They learn to work with joy by seeing adults who serve without complaining.

Joy in serving does not mean every task is fun. It means you remember who you are serving. You are serving the Lord. Folding laundry, cooking meals, cleaning up messes, helping a sibling, all of these are spiritual when done with the right heart.

This week, talk about gifts. Not talents only. Spiritual gifts come from God for building others up. Some teach. Some lead. Some show mercy. Some encourage. Some give. Some organize. Some offer help quietly. Help each family member see how their gift can be used.

Then take one step. As a family, plan one act of service. Help a neighbor. Serve at church. Clean for someone who is sick. Write a letter to someone discouraged. Let each person contribute in their own way. Keep the goal simple. Serve with care. Serve with joy.

Also serve inside your home. Make a list of everyday ways to bless each other. Do one per day. Rotate the names. The one who usually leads should step back. The one who usually receives should step forward. Let everyone practice giving.

Do not link service to reward. Joy is the reward. Train your family to say, "I serve because God served me first." Use that phrase often.

Watch your attitude. If someone grumbles while helping, pause. Reset. Remind them who they're serving. If pride creeps in, correct gently. Remind your family that service done to be noticed loses its purpose.

At the end of the week, gather and review what happened. Ask each person, "What did you learn from serving?" Keep answers short and sincere. Then pray together. Thank God for using your family.

Faithful service often feels small. It looks like wiping a table. Making a meal. Listening without interrupting. It feels quiet, but it matters. God sees. God multiplies the impact.

Keep serving. Keep watching for needs. Keep using your gifts. That's the life of a steward. That's the life of joy.

Discussion Questions

1. What gift has God given you to serve others?
2. How can your family serve someone together this week?
3. What attitude helps you serve with joy?
4. How will you remind yourself who you are serving?

Family Prayer

God, thank You for giving us gifts. Help us use them well. Teach us to serve with joy, not pride or complaint. Open our eyes to the needs around us. Let our family be faithful with what You've given. In Jesus' name. Amen.

Week 36: Giving Cheerfully

"Each one must give as he has decided in his heart, not reluctantly or under compulsion, for God loves a cheerful giver." – 2 Corinthians 9:7

Giving is not a rule to follow. It is a choice made from the heart. God does not want gifts given with guilt. He wants gifts given with joy. The Bible makes this clear. God loves a cheerful giver.

This verse gives three instructions. Decide in your heart. Do not give under pressure. Give with joy. These steps help families learn how to give with the right attitude.

Giving starts with a decision. You must think about it ahead of time. You must plan for it. You must choose it on purpose. That means your family talks about giving before the moment comes. Giving becomes part of your life, not something left to chance.

Next, giving must be free. No one should force you. That includes leaders, teachers, or parents. Giving is not a way to earn favor with God. You already have His love through Christ. You give because you're thankful. You give because it honors Him.

Joy in giving grows with practice. At first, it may feel hard. You may want to keep what you have, but as your family learns to trust God's provision, giving becomes a joy. You begin to see how your gifts bless others. You begin to care more about people than things.

Teach your children how giving works. Give them small amounts to manage. Show them how to divide it: some to save, some to give, some to use. Let them choose where to give. Let them feel the cost. Then let them feel the joy.

This week, set a giving goal as a family. Choose an amount. Choose a person, family, church, or ministry to receive it. Make the gift together. Pray before giving. Give it quietly. Do not seek praise. God sees.

Also teach giving through time and effort. Giving is not only about money. You give when you help someone move. You give when you make a meal. You give when you share what you have. You give when you show up for someone who is struggling.

Guard your heart from two dangers. First is pride. Do not give to feel better than others. Second is fear. Do not hold back because you think you will run out. God provides. Your job is to give with open hands and trust Him.

At the end of the week, ask each person one question: "What did giving teach you?" Keep answers short and honest. Giving forms your heart. Over time, it shapes how your home views money, people, and trust in God.

Discussion Questions

1. What makes giving hard sometimes?
2. How does it feel different to give cheerfully instead of out of guilt?
3. What will your family give this week, and to whom?
4. What other ways, besides money, can you give?

Family Prayer

God, thank You for giving to us first. Help us give with joy, not pressure. Keep us from pride. Keep us from fear. Use our gifts to help others and honor You. Teach our family to live with open hands and trusting hearts. In Jesus' name. Amen.

Week 37: Walking in Unity

"Make every effort to keep the unity of the Spirit through the bond of peace." – Ephesians 4:3

Unity does not happen by accident. Families drift toward conflict, not peace. God tells you to work for unity. Not once. Not occasionally. Every effort. That means daily choices, not quick fixes.

Unity comes from the Spirit, not from agreement on every detail. You will have different opinions. You will face tension. The goal is not perfect sameness. The goal is shared direction under God's Word.

Start with tone. A harsh tone breaks unity fast. A mocking tone destroys trust. A quiet, steady tone builds peace. In your home, decide now: your words will aim for peace. That does not mean avoiding truth. It means speaking with care.

Next, set shared habits. Read Scripture together. Pray together. Share meals. Ask each person how they are doing. These moments build connections. Disconnection leads to distance. Distance leads to division.

Watch how you handle mistakes. When someone fails, do you shame or restore? When someone confesses, do you punish or forgive? Unity grows when grace and truth stay balanced. No one gets ignored. No one gets crushed.

This week, choose one unity practice. Pick one: listening without interrupting, finishing hard talks without walking away, or praying together after conflict. Keep the practice simple. Repeat it daily.

Unity also means carrying shared burdens. When one person is stressed, the others help. When one person feels alone, the others draw near. Ask each day, "How can I help you today?" Small helps build strong unity.

When conflict happens, and it will, respond early. Do not let offense sit. Speak clearly. Admit sin. Forgive fast. Take one repair step. Then move forward. Let peace return quickly.

Do not demand unity from others without showing it yourself. Parents must model what they expect. Children must be trained, not forced. Teens must be given room to grow, not room to divide.

Unity is not silent. Unity means you speak hard truths without breaking the bond. You protect relationships while holding each other to God's standard.

Use this sentence often: "We are one family, serving one Lord." Write it on paper. Say it before hard conversations. Let it shape your reactions.

At the end of the week, gather and review. Each person answers one question: "What helped our family grow in unity this week?" Keep answers brief. Celebrate progress. Plan one next step.

Unity is fragile when ignored. Unity is strong when guarded. Make every effort. God gives peace to families who walk in obedience.

Discussion Questions

1. What weakens unity in your home?
2. What action brings peace after tension?
3. What shared habit will your family practice this week?
4. How does your tone affect unity?

Family Prayer

Father, help our family walk in unity. Keep us from harsh words and selfish plans. Teach us to forgive quickly and speak with care. Show us how to protect the peace You give. Make us one through Your Spirit. In Jesus' name. Amen.

Week 38: Living by the Spirit

"For those who are led by the Spirit of God are the children of God." - Romans 8:14

God's children do not live by impulse. They live by direction. That direction comes from the Holy Spirit. He does not shout. He leads. If you belong to God, the Spirit leads your choices, your reactions, your words, and your plans.

Living by the Spirit means you are not controlled by sin. You do not follow every craving. You do not return to old habits without resistance. You walk in step with what pleases God. This does not mean you never fail. It means you do not settle into sin. You listen. You repent. You obey.

Start with awareness. The Spirit speaks through Scripture. He brings verses to mind. He convicts when you drift. He strengthens when you feel weak. He helps you say no to pride, anger, fear, and greed. He helps you say yes to peace, truth, and love.

Teach your family to recognize His leading. When someone feels torn between two options, pause and ask: "What does God's Word say?" The Spirit will never lead you to sin. He will never lead you to selfishness. He leads toward obedience.

This week, train your home to ask one question before decisions: "What would the Spirit lead me to do here?" Write this question on a card and keep it visible. Use it before speaking in conflict, before spending, before reacting, before quitting.

The Spirit leads differently in each moment. One person may be led to wait. Another may be led to act. The test is always the same: does this match Scripture? Does this reflect Christ? Does this honor God?

At home, the Spirit may lead you to hold your tongue when tension rises. He may lead you to offer help before being asked. He may lead you to confess a sin you hoped to ignore. Follow fast. Do not delay. Delayed obedience grows dullness. Quick obedience strengthens hearing.

Children can be taught this too. When emotions rise, teach them to stop and pray, "Holy Spirit, help me obey." When they are unsure, teach them to ask, "What would God want me to do now?" These patterns grow early sensitivity to God's leadership.

Living by the Spirit brings peace. It does not remove trouble, but it removes confusion. You no longer guess what is right. You are no longer ruled by pressure. You listen and obey. Over time, the fruit of the Spirit grows in your home.

Keep a record this week. Each evening, have each person name one time they followed the Spirit's lead. Keep answers short. Celebrate growth. When someone fails, respond with grace and truth. Confess. Reset. Keep walking.

Discussion Questions

1. What does it mean to be led by the Spirit?
2. When have you felt the Spirit guiding you?
3. What helps you tell the difference between His voice and your own feelings?
4. What habit this week will help your family follow the Spirit more closely?

Family Prayer

Holy Spirit, lead our family. Teach us to listen and obey. Show us what honors God. Help us turn away from sin and walk in truth. Grow Your fruit in our lives. Make our home peaceful and faithful as we follow You. In Jesus' name. Amen.

Week 39: Seeking God's Kingdom

"But seek first the kingdom of God and his righteousness, and all these things will be added to you." – Matthew 6:33

Jesus spoke these words to people worried about their needs: food, clothes, and daily life. He did not tell them their needs didn't matter. He told them what matters most. Seek God's kingdom first. Everything else comes after.

Seeking God's kingdom means putting His rule above your own. It means His Word sets the direction. His will shapes your plans. His priorities become your family's priorities.

You must choose what comes first. Many families chase comfort, success, or approval. These are not always wrong, but when they come first, God's kingdom gets pushed aside. This verse calls your home to realignment.

Start with the word seek. Seeking is active. It takes effort. You do not seek by chance. You seek with purpose. You open Scripture daily. You pray before decisions. You ask, "What does God want us to do right now?"

Next is the word first. Not later. Not when everything else is finished. Not when you feel like it. First means God's way comes before your preferences, your habits, and your schedule. First means God gets the best, not the leftovers.

Your children must see what "seek first" looks like in real time. That means worship on Sunday matters more than sports. It means giving comes before spending. It means truth matters more than comfort. They watch your decisions. They copy your priorities.

This week, make one family plan. Each person chooses one area to seek God first. One person may pray before school. One may start the day in Scripture. One may set a new limit on entertainment. Keep it specific and daily. Write it down.

Also look at your calendar. What does your schedule say about your priorities? What do you say yes to most often? What do you rush through or cancel? Adjust what needs adjusting. Seeking God first requires structure.

Do not fear missing out. Jesus said when you seek His kingdom first, God will provide what you need. He did not promise luxury. He promised provision. Your job is to obey. His job is to supply.

At the end of each day, ask one question: "Did we seek God's kingdom today?" Keep answers honest and brief. If you missed the mark, confess. Then reset for tomorrow.

The world will not push you toward the kingdom. It will distract you from it. Stay focused. Stay faithful.

Discussion Questions

1. What does seeking God's kingdom look like in daily life?
2. What often takes first place in your schedule?
3. What action will you take this week to put God first?
4. How does this verse change your view of worry?

Family Prayer

Father, help us seek Your kingdom first. Show us what to say no to. Show us what to say yes to. Teach us to trust You with our needs. Let our home follow Your ways and Your priorities. In Jesus' name. Amen.

Week 40: Standing on Truth

"Then you will know the truth, and the truth will set you free." - John 8:32

Truth does not change. Feelings shift. Culture shifts. Opinions shift, but God's truth stays firm. Jesus said when you know the truth, it brings freedom. Lies trap. Truth frees.

In a family, truth must lead. Not feelings. Not pressure. Not comfort. Truth must decide how you speak, how you correct, how you lead, and how you live. That starts with Scripture. The Bible is God's truth, not opinion. It is clear. It is enough.

This verse comes from Jesus' teaching. He told people to stay in His word. Then they would be His disciples. Then they would know the truth. Then they would be free. Freedom follows obedience. Obedience starts with knowing.

This means you must train your family in the Word. Do not depend on others to teach your children the truth. Make it normal in your home. Use short readings. Use questions. Use conversation. Speak about truth when life feels confusing. Go back to Scripture when decisions feel unclear.

Truth must shape correction. When someone sins, speak truth calmly. When someone fails, point them back to what God says. Do not correct based on moods or convenience. Use clear verses. Say, "God says we must speak truth." Say, "God says we must forgive." Use truth, not emotion.

Truth also protects against lies. The world will speak loudly. It will call sin good. It will tell your children to follow their feelings. It will pressure your teens to hide faith. Truth gives your family the strength to stand. Do not soften it. Do not twist it to fit in. Say what is true. Stand firm.

This week, choose one truth your family needs to remember. Write it down. Say it daily. For example: "God made us for His glory." Or, "God is always with us." Or, "Jesus is the only way." Keep the statement short. Root it in Scripture.

Also correct one lie. Ask each person: "What lie do you hear most often?" It may be "I have to be perfect," or "I am not valuable," or "Sin won't hurt me." Then speak the truth that replaces the lie. Say it out loud.

Help your children practice this too. Teach them to ask: "Is this true?" before they repeat something, believe something, or share something online. Truth-checking becomes a lifelong habit.

At the end of each day, ask: "Where did we stand on truth today?" Keep answers short. Be honest. If truth was ignored, correct it. If truth was spoken, give thanks.

Standing on truth will not always make you popular, but it will make you steady. God honors families who do not bend.

Discussion Questions

1. What is one truth your family needs to hold to right now?
2. What lie do you need to stop believing?
3. How does knowing God's Word help you stand firm?
4. What habit can help your family keep truth in view each day?

Family Prayer

Lord, thank You for truth that does not change. Help us stand on it. Protect us from lies. Train our hearts and mouths to stay faithful to Your Word. Give us courage to speak truth and to live it. In Jesus' name. Amen.

Part 5: Hope and Perseverance

Week 41: Enduring Trials

"Blessed is the one who perseveres under trial because, having stood the test, that person will receive the crown of life that the Lord has promised to those who love him." – James 1:12

Trials are part of life. They come in many forms: sickness, loss, disappointment, pressure, or pain. God does not promise to remove every trial. He promises strength to endure. He promises reward to those who remain faithful.

This verse gives a clear goal: perseverance. That means you do not quit when things feel heavy. You do not run when things get hard. You stay steady. You keep obeying God, even when the outcome is slow or unclear.

Perseverance does not mean you enjoy the trial. It means you keep going through it with faith. You keep showing up to pray. You keep doing what is right. You keep trusting God's Word. This is how your faith grows strong.

James says the one who endures is blessed. Not because of the pain, but because of what God produces through it. Trials test your heart. They reveal what you trust. They show whether your faith is rooted in comfort or in Christ.

Talk openly as a family about the trials you face. Name them. Speak them with calm, not fear. When you hide trials, they grow in silence. When you bring them into the light, you make room for support, prayer, and steady obedience.

This week, choose one trial your family is facing. It could be a hard relationship, a financial need, a health concern, or daily stress. Write it down. Pray over it each day. Ask God for strength, not escape. Ask for obedience, not ease.

Teach your children that hard days do not mean God has left. Remind them that Jesus suffered too. He endured the cross with joy because He knew the purpose. Endurance looks ahead to the reward God promised: eternal life with Him.

Set a perseverance plan. When discouragement rises, you stop and pray. You read one verse aloud. You speak one sentence of truth. You take one small step forward. These habits build endurance.

At the end of the week, talk about what helped. Ask each person: "What did you learn about God during this trial?" Keep the focus on faith, not comfort. Celebrate obedience, not ease.

When someone feels like giving up, gather around them. Speak Scripture. Serve with quiet help. Pray without long speeches. Endurance grows stronger in a faithful home.

Discussion Questions

1. What trial is your family walking through right now?
2. What helps you stay faithful when life feels hard?
3. How can you support each other in perseverance?
4. What promise from God gives you strength to keep going?

Family Prayer

Lord, You see the trials we face. Help us endure with faith. Strengthen our hearts when we feel weak. Keep us steady when we feel tired. Let our home trust You more, not less, in hardship. Thank You for the crown of life You promise. In Jesus' name. Amen.

Week 42: God's Strength in Weakness

"But he said to me, 'My grace is sufficient for you, for my power is made perfect in weakness.' Therefore I will boast all the more gladly of my weaknesses, so that the power of Christ may rest upon me." - 2 Corinthians 12:9

Weakness is not something most people want to admit. In families, weakness often looks like tiredness, frustration, doubt, or failure.

God does not reject the weak. He works through them. His strength shows up when yours runs out.

Paul wrote these words after asking God to remove a painful problem. God did not remove it. Instead, He gave something better: grace. God told Paul, "My grace is enough." That is still true today.

This verse reminds your family that weakness is not the end. It is the starting point for God's strength. You do not have to hide your struggle. You do not have to act like everything is fine. You bring your weakness to God, and He gives power.

God's power is not shown through pride or self-sufficiency. It is shown through humility and surrender. When your children see you admit weakness and trust God anyway, they learn to do the same. This creates honesty, not performance, in your home.

This week, talk about what feels hard. Each person shares one area of weakness. Maybe it's fear, anxiety, anger, impatience, or physical tiredness. Keep it simple. Do not fix. Do not shame. Just speak it. Then say together, "God's grace is enough."

Next, ask how Christ's power could rest on that weakness. That may mean more prayer. More Scripture. More rest. More boundaries. More help from others. God does not always remove the burden, but He always provides strength to keep walking.

Teach your children that weakness is not failure. Weakness is part of life. You feel weak when you obey even when you are tired. You feel weak when you do not know what to do. That's when you pray. That's when God supplies strength.

Choose one action as a family this week. When someone feels weak, pause. Speak this verse out loud. Pray one sentence: "Jesus, give us Your strength." Then take one step forward. Keep the focus on grace, not performance.

Also talk about what strength in Christ looks like. It is calm under pressure. It is obedience in hard moments. It is kindness when you feel irritated. It is faith when answers do not come fast.

Write the verse somewhere visible this week. Let it be a reminder: you do not have to carry everything alone.

Discussion Questions

1. Where do you feel weak right now?
2. How does it help to know God's strength shows up in weakness?
3. What can you do when a family member feels overwhelmed?
4. What does it look like to rely on grace instead of personal strength?

Family Prayer

Lord, we feel weak in many ways. Thank You for meeting us there. Teach us to stop pretending. Teach us to depend on You. Show us Your strength when we feel empty. Let our family live by grace, not pride. In Jesus' name. Amen.

Week 43: Waiting with Patience

"Wait for the Lord; be strong, and let your heart take courage; wait for the Lord!" - Psalm 27:14

Waiting is never easy. You pray, but the answer doesn't come. You plan, but the door stays closed. You hope, but time keeps moving. Waiting tests the heart. It also builds it, when done with patience and trust.

David wrote this verse during a season of fear and uncertainty. He didn't say, "Get what you want fast." He said, "Wait for the Lord." That means you wait with your eyes on God, not on the clock.

Waiting does not mean doing nothing. Waiting means you stay faithful while the outcome is unclear. You keep praying. You keep obeying. You keep choosing trust over panic. That's what it means to wait with strength.

Patience is not passive. It is active trust. It says, "God is working, even if I don't see how." It says, "I will not rush ahead or give up." In a family, patience shows in words, tone, and choices. Children must be taught that delay is not the same as denial.

This week, talk as a family about what you are waiting for. Healing. Clarity. Change. Provision. Write down one thing for each person. Then pray together, "God, help us wait with faith." Keep the list visible. Review it at the end of the week.

Use this time to train your hearts. When frustration rises, pause and pray. Say out loud, "God sees. God knows. We will wait on Him." These sentences are short, but they reset the moment.

Also train in small ways. If a child complains about waiting, guide them toward calm. If a teen wants quick results, help them build a plan. If a parent feels tired of waiting, speak truth gently: God does not forget His people.

Encourage each other through Scripture. Read one Psalm each night. Let God's Word remind you of His faithfulness. Say together, "God has never failed His people. He won't fail us now."

At the end of each day, ask: "How did we wait with trust today?" Keep answers short. Celebrate effort. Don't shame mistakes. Waiting well is learned over time.

When answers come, give thanks. Tell the story. Let your children see that God's timing is better than your own. Let them learn that patient hearts are strong hearts.

Discussion Questions

1. What are you waiting on God for right now?
2. What makes waiting hard?
3. How can your family support each other patiently?
4. What truth will help you stay calm while you wait?

Family Prayer

Lord, we don't always like to wait. Help us trust You when answers seem far away. Strengthen our hearts. Remind us that You are near. Teach our family to wait with patience, not fear. We choose to trust You today. In Jesus' name. Amen.

Week 44: Finding Rest in Christ

"Come to me, all who labor and are heavy laden, and I will give you rest." - Matthew 11:28

Jesus gives an open invitation. He speaks to the tired. He calls to the overwhelmed. He offers rest, not escape, not distraction, but real rest for the soul. That promise still stands today.

This rest is not a vacation or a break from responsibility. It is peace in the middle of pressure. It is calm in the middle of noise. It is confidence that you don't carry life alone. Jesus says, "Come to me." Rest starts with turning to Him.

Many families live in constant motion. School. Work. Schedules. Chores. Screens. Stress builds up. You feel like there's no space to stop, but if you do not make space to rest in Christ, your strength runs out. This kind of tired is not solved by sleep alone. It's a heart issue.

Jesus does not give a long list of steps. He gives a person: Himself. Come to Me. That means pray. That means stop and read His Word. That means pause and speak His name. That means trust that He knows what you carry and that He's not asking you to carry it alone.

Talk as a family about what feels heavy. Ask, "What are you tired of carrying?" Write it down. Then read this verse together. Let each person speak a short prayer, offering their burden to Jesus. Keep it simple. Keep it real.

Also make one plan for rest. Choose one time this week to stop and be quiet together. No phones. No tasks. Just read one Psalm. Sit together. Pray one sentence each. Let that space remind you that Jesus gives rest to those who come.

Teach your children that rest is not weakness. Rest is obedience. Even God rested after creation. Jesus rested during ministry. Rest is part of a faithful life. It shows trust. It shows humility.

Watch for signs of restlessness in your home: short tempers, constant complaining, exhaustion, or withdrawal. These are signals. Respond with calm. Invite the family back to Jesus, not into more activity.

At the end of the week, ask: "Where did we find rest in Christ?" Celebrate even small steps. Encourage each other to keep the habit. Real rest becomes a pattern, not a one-time fix.

Jesus is not distant from your stress. He is near. He invites you to come. Say yes. Again and again.

Discussion Questions

1. What makes you feel burdened right now?
2. How do you usually try to rest? Does it help?
3. What does it look like to come to Jesus with your stress?
4. What habit will your family change this week to make space for rest?

Family Prayer

Jesus, thank You for inviting us to come to You. We are tired. We carry too much. We try to do too much on our own. Teach us to rest in You. Quiet our hearts. Remind us that You are near. Give our family peace and strength through Your presence. Amen.

Week 45: The Peace of God

"Peace I leave with you; my peace I give to you. Not as the world gives do I give to you. Let not your hearts be troubled, neither let them be afraid." - John 14:27

Jesus spoke these words before facing the cross. He knew fear would rise in His disciples. He knew trouble would come.

He also knew the peace He gives is different. Stronger. Steady. Not based on comfort, but on His presence.

The world offers peace that depends on the situation. When things feel calm, peace is possible. When plans break or pressure comes, peace disappears.

The peace of God does not change. It stays, even in chaos.

This peace is not the absence of problems. It is the presence of Christ. That's why Jesus says, "My peace I give to you." It's not something you earn. It's not something you fake. It is a gift He gives.

Peace must be received. That means you trust God instead of your fear. You stop trying to control everything. You slow your words. You speak His truth aloud. You return to prayer before reacting.

Families feel the need for peace in real ways. Busy schedules. Health problems. Conflict at home. Strained finances. Tired hearts. These moments expose where your peace comes from. Let them lead you back to Jesus, not deeper into stress.

This week, name what is troubling your hearts. Each person writes down one concern. Then read this verse out loud. Let it replace fear. Let it shape your next step. Say together, "Jesus, give us Your peace."

Use Scripture to speak peace over your home. Choose one verse each day and read it aloud. Post it in a visible place. Let God's Word settle your tone, your pace, and your responses.

Train your children to pray in stressful moments. Simple words. "Jesus, help me trust You." "Give me Your peace." These habits matter. They build strong hearts in uncertain days.

Also create a reset plan. When tension rises in your home, stop for thirty seconds. Take one deep breath. Say one truth. Speak one prayer. Then continue with calm. Over time, this becomes a pattern of peace.

God's peace doesn't always change the outside situation, but it changes your heart. It helps you respond instead of react. It helps you love instead of panic. It keeps your family grounded in what is true.

Discussion Questions

1. What tends to trouble your heart most often?
2. What does it mean that Jesus gives peace "not as the world gives"?
3. How can your family pause and reset when stress rises?
4. What will help you choose peace this week?

Family Prayer

Jesus, thank You for giving us Your peace. Help us to receive it, trust it, and live in it. Quiet our hearts when we feel afraid. Slow our minds when we feel rushed. Let Your peace shape our words and guide our home. In Your name, Amen.

Week 46: Hope in God's Promises

"May the God of hope fill you with all joy and peace in believing, so that by the power of the Holy Spirit you may abound in hope." – Romans 15:13

Hope does not come from feelings. It comes from belief in God's promises. When your faith rests on what God has said, hope grows. Even when circumstances feel dark, hope remains steady.

This verse reminds you where hope starts. It starts with God. He is the God of hope. He is not limited by what you see. He is not delayed by what troubles you. He is faithful to every word He speaks.

Paul prays for believers to be filled with joy and peace in believing. That means you do not wait for everything to improve before trusting God. You believe now. You trust while you wait. You hold to His promises when answers feel slow.

Hope is not pretending everything is fine. Hope is knowing God is in control even when nothing feels fine. That kind of hope only comes through the Holy Spirit. You cannot force it. You ask for it. You receive it. Then you walk in it.

This week, talk as a family about where hope feels low. Maybe it's a situation that hasn't changed. Maybe it's a need that feels too big. Write it down. Then read this verse aloud. Ask God to fill that place with His hope.

Also review the promises of God. Make a short list together. Choose three promises from Scripture. For example:

God is with us (Matthew 28:20)

God hears our prayers (1 John 5:14)

God works all things for good (Romans 8:28)

Write these down. Say them out loud each day. Let truth rebuild what discouragement has broken.

Hope shapes how you speak. Use words that reflect trust. Say, "God is working." Say, "We're waiting with faith." These words shape your home. They teach your children what it means to walk by belief, not by sight.

When someone in the family feels discouraged, stop and pray together. Keep it short. "God, fill us with hope." Do not offer shallow answers. Sit together. Point back to the truth. Let peace grow from Scripture, not opinion.

At the end of the week, ask: "Where did we see hope grow?" Celebrate small steps. Speak thanks to God. Hope often grows quietly. Over time, it becomes strong.

God does not break His promises. He will finish what He started. Teach your family to build their hope on that truth.

Discussion Questions

1. Where do you feel low on hope right now?
2. What promise from God helps you trust Him?
3. How does the Holy Spirit help you hope in hard times?
4. What habit can your family start to grow hope this week?

Family Prayer

God of hope, fill us with Your joy and peace. Teach us to trust Your promises. Strengthen our faith when we feel weak. Help our family live with hope that does not depend on feelings. Let Your Spirit keep us steady and full of trust. In Jesus' name. Amen.

Week 47: Joy in the Lord

"Do not grieve, for the joy of the Lord is your strength." – Nehemiah 8:10

Joy is not the same as happiness. Happiness depends on how things are going. Joy comes from the Lord. It stays even when life feels hard. It gives strength when you feel tired, uncertain, or overwhelmed.

This verse was spoken to God's people after they heard His Word and wept. They realized how far they had fallen.

Nehemiah reminded them: this was not a moment for grief. This was a moment to return to God with joy.

The people had repented. Now they were to respond with worship and gladness. Why? Because God had not left them. He had spoken. He had gathered them. And He would be their strength again.

Your family needs this same reminder. When mistakes are confessed and truth is spoken, joy can return. It's not fake. It's not forced. It's the steady joy of knowing God is near and faithful.

This week, talk about where joy feels low. Maybe it's a long week, a disappointment, or something that didn't go as planned. Name it. Then return to this truth: "The joy of the Lord is our strength."

Joy grows when you remember what God has done. Set aside one time this week to name His goodness. Each person lists three things God has provided, past or present. Meals. Safety. Help. Grace. Make the list together. Then give thanks in prayer.

Also remember that joy often follows obedience. When your family reads Scripture, confesses sin, prays together, and walks in faith, joy follows. It may not be loud, but it is deep. And it strengthens the home.

Use this sentence often: "We choose joy today." Say it before the day begins. Say it when stress shows up. Say it when tempers rise. This keeps your hearts anchored in what matters most.

Don't confuse joy with ignoring hard things. The people in Nehemiah's time faced real challenges, but they were told to find strength in God's joy. You can do the same.

At the end of the week, ask, "Where did we see God's joy give us strength?" Let each person answer. Keep it short. Give thanks together.

Discussion Questions

1. What makes it hard to feel joy right now?
2. What is one thing God has done for your family this week?
3. How does the joy of the Lord give strength in hard moments?
4. What habit will help your home choose joy each day?

Family Prayer

Lord, thank You for being our joy. When we feel tired or discouraged, remind us of Your presence. Fill our home with Your peace. Teach us to give thanks and remember Your goodness. Let Your joy be our strength today. In Jesus' name. Amen.

Week 48: God's Faithfulness

"The steadfast love of the Lord never ceases; his mercies never come to an end; they are new every morning; great is your faithfulness." – Lamentations 3:22-23

These words were written during deep sorrow. Jerusalem was in ruins. The people were suffering. Yet in the middle of pain, this truth rose: God's faithfulness never fails. His mercy returns every day. He does not grow tired. He does not forget.

God's faithfulness means He keeps His promises. Every time. Not once. Not sometimes. Every time. He does what He says. He shows love that does not stop. He gives mercy that does not run out.

This is the foundation your family can build on. When circumstances change. When people disappoint. When plans fall apart. God remains steady. His love is still there in the morning.

Help your children understand that God's faithfulness is not the same as getting what you want. It means He is present. He is trustworthy. He provides what you need when you need it, even if the path looks different than expected.

This week, talk as a family about where you've seen God's faithfulness. Make a list. Go back as far as you can remember. Look for answered prayers. Unexpected help. Strength in weakness. Peace in trouble. Write them down and say, "God was faithful here."

Choose one moment from the past when your family faced hardship. Talk about what happened. Then ask, "How did God show His faithfulness?" Let your children hear the full story. Let them see how God worked in the middle of it.

Also practice looking ahead. When facing something uncertain now, speak the truth: "God will be faithful again." Teach your family to pray with confidence, not fear. Teach them to expect mercy in the morning, because He said it would come.

Make a visual reminder this week. On a piece of paper, write "Great is Your faithfulness." Place it where everyone can see it. When tension rises or hearts grow tired, point back to that truth.

If someone feels discouraged, gently remind them of who God is. Do not rush past their emotions.

Do not stay stuck in it. Speak the verse. Pray together. Let God's Word lead the moment.

Faithfulness is who God is. It does not depend on your effort. It does not rise and fall with your mood. It remains steady. That's why you can rest.

Discussion Questions

1. Where has God shown faithfulness to our family in the past?
2. How does God's faithfulness help us face the future?
3. What promise of God brings you peace today?
4. How can we remind each other of His mercy each morning?

Family Prayer

Father, thank You for being faithful. When we change, You stay the same. When we forget, You remember. When we grow tired, You remain strong. Help us trust Your mercy each morning. Let our family rest in Your love. In Jesus' name. Amen.

Week 49: Eternal Perspective

"Set your minds on things that are above, not on things that are on earth." – Colossians 3:2

Your thoughts shape your priorities. Where your mind stays, your heart follows. That's why Paul commands believers to set their minds on things above. Not once in a while. Not when life slows down. Every day.

Eternal perspective means you live with forever in view. You remember that this life is short. You focus on what will still matter a thousand years from now. You hold loosely to things that fade. You hold tightly to the Word of God.

Many families get stuck in daily pressure, such as appointments, chores, plans, and stress. These things matter, but they are not the center. The center is Christ. When your thoughts rise above the moment, peace grows. Clarity returns. Hope resets.

This verse calls your family to think about God's promises, not just your to-do list. Think about heaven. Think about righteousness. Think about the truth. Think about what pleases the Lord. That mindset shapes how you spend time, how you speak, and how you respond to trouble.

This week, name three things that tend to take up too much of your family's focus. Write them down. Then ask, "Will this still matter in eternity?" If the answer is no, loosen your grip. Let God realign your priorities.

Also name three eternal things that deserve more focus. Prayer. Scripture. Forgiveness. Serving others. These things carry weight beyond this life. Make a plan to give one of them more time this week.

Teach your children that life is not random. It has a direction. God made them with purpose. He called them to live for more than comfort, attention, or things. Let that truth shape their identity.

Use short phrases throughout the day to shift your thinking. Say, "This moment is temporary." Say, "We're living for what lasts." Say, "Jesus is the goal." These words help your family stay grounded when emotions run high.

Eternal perspective also changes how you handle loss, delay, and disappointment. When plans fall through, you can say, "God sees the whole picture." When things go well, you can say, "This blessing points us back to God."

At the end of the week, talk as a family. Ask: "What helped us think about eternal things this week?" Keep answers short. Stay honest. Celebrate growth, even if small.

Discussion Questions

1. What daily things distract you from thinking about God?
2. What helps you keep an eternal mindset?
3. How can your family remind each other to live for what matters most?
4. What habit will you start this week to set your mind on things above?

Family Prayer

Father, help us set our minds on what is above. Train our thoughts. Reset our focus. Teach us to live with eternity in view. Help our home care more about Your truth than temporary things. Keep us faithful to You. In Jesus' name. Amen.

Week 50: Trusting God's Timing

"For everything there is a season, and a time for every matter under heaven." – Ecclesiastes 3:1

God is never late. He is never rushed. He does not miss details. He does not forget His people. This verse reminds us that everything has a season, and God is the one who sets the times.

Trusting God's timing means you stop trying to force your own. You don't rush what He's not ready to give. You don't panic when things feel slow. You rest in His wisdom, even when the wait feels long.

Every family walks through seasons. Some feel full of progress and joy. Others feel quiet, confusing, or hard. You may want to skip ahead, but God uses every season to grow your faith. None of them are wasted.

Teach your family that God sees the full picture. You see one moment at a time. He sees the beginning, middle, and end. When you trust His timing, you walk with peace. You stop trying to control what is not yours to control.

This week, name the season your family is in. Are you waiting for something? Facing change? Feeling loss? Starting something new? Write it down. Then say together, "We will trust God with this season."

Also name one area where you feel rushed or impatient. It could be a decision, a plan, or a prayer request. Instead of pushing harder, choose one action of faith: read a verse, pray, or serve someone. Let obedience replace pressure.

Make a family habit this week: each night, answer the question, "What is God teaching us in this season?" Keep answers short. Be honest. Look for small signs of growth. Don't wait for big changes to give thanks.

God's timing also includes His work in others. Be patient with each other. Let your children grow at their own pace. Let your spouse change over time. Let your home be a place where grace and truth work side by side.

When delays come, remind each other: "There is a time for every matter under heaven." That includes sorrow, rest, laughter, hard work, and healing. God holds it all. Your job is to walk faithfully in the season He has placed you.

Discussion Questions

1. What season does our family seem to be in right now?
2. Where are we tempted to rush ahead of God?
3. How does trusting God's timing change our attitude?
4. What habit can help us stay steady in this season?

Family Prayer

Lord, You know the times and seasons. You do not make mistakes. Help us trust You with what we do not understand. Teach us to walk with peace and patience. Use this season to grow our faith. Let our family wait with hope and obey with joy. In Jesus' name. Amen.

Part 6: Family Legacy of Faith

Week 51: Generations of Blessing

"But the steadfast love of the Lord is from everlasting to everlasting on those who fear him, and his righteousness to children's children." - Psalm 103:17

God thinks in generations. His love does not stop with one person. It reaches through time: grandparents, parents, children, and beyond. When a family fears the Lord and walks in His ways, the blessing spreads farther than they can see.

This verse reminds you that faith in the home is not only about today. It's about what your children will carry into adulthood. It's about what they will pass on to their children. When you obey God now, you shape the future.

The "steadfast love of the Lord" is His covenant love. It is loyal, secure, and lasting. It does not fade. It does not depend on how you feel. It comes from God's character, and He pours it out on those who fear Him.

To fear the Lord means to honor Him above all. It means you obey Him when it's hard. You repent when you sin. You raise your children to know His truth. This posture invites His blessing. It also sets the tone for the generations that follow.

This week, talk about the spiritual heritage in your family. Has faith been passed down? Are you beginning that legacy now? Speak honestly. Whether you're continuing a strong legacy or starting something new, God meets you with mercy and strength.

Make a list of one spiritual habit your family wants to pass on: daily prayer, Sunday worship, forgiveness, Scripture reading, or giving. Pick one and practice it with care this week. Do it faithfully. Your consistency teaches more than your words.

Also write down one prayer for the next generation. Pray aloud for your children and their children. Pray they will love God, walk in truth, and serve Him with joy. Let your children hear that prayer. Let them feel the weight and the hope of it.

Children need to know they are part of something bigger. God's story did not start with them, and it won't end with them. Help them see their place in a line of people who trust and follow the Lord.

At the end of the week, reflect as a family: "What are we building that will last beyond us?" Keep answers simple. Let this shape your goals. Let it guide how you spend time and what you say yes to.

Discussion Questions

1. What faith habits do you want to pass down?
2. How has God's love shown up across generations in your family?
3. What choices now will bless the people who come after us?
4. What prayer do you want to speak over the next generation?

Family Prayer

Lord, thank You for loving us with an everlasting love. Help us walk in Your ways. Let our obedience bless our children and their children. Build a lasting faith in our home. Make our family part of Your work through the generations. In Jesus' name. Amen.

Week 52: A Family That Serves the Lord

"But as for me and my house, we will serve the Lord." - Joshua 24:15

At the end of his life, Joshua gathered the people and made a clear choice. He reminded them of God's faithfulness. Then he said something bold. No matter what others did, his family would serve the Lord. It was personal. It was public. It was final.

Every family must choose who they will serve. Culture pushes families to chase success, comfort, and ease.

The call of God remains the same: serve the Lord. Not just in words, but in actions. Not once, but every day.

Serving the Lord means putting Him first in your home. It means you follow His Word, even when it costs you something. It means you forgive when it's hard. You tell the truth when it's risky. You say yes to His ways and no to the world's lies.

This choice is not made in one moment. It is made in patterns. In tone. In priorities. In how you spend your time and what you celebrate. When a family serves the Lord, it becomes visible.

This week, ask each person in your home: "What does it look like for us to serve the Lord together?" Let the answers guide your week. Maybe it's reading Scripture daily. Maybe it's helping someone in need. Maybe it's ending a habit that doesn't honor God. Pick one step and take it.

Write down the sentence from Joshua: "As for me and my house, we will serve the Lord." Place it where your family can see it. Let it shape your decisions. Let it remind you what your home stands for.

Serving the Lord does not mean perfection. It means repentance. When your family fails, return quickly. Confess sin. Forgive one another. Get back on the path. That is part of service too.

If your children are young, teach them simple habits. Speak God's name aloud. Pray before choices. Serve with gladness. If they are older, challenge them to think about their future: how they will lead and how they will follow.

As this year ends, reflect as a family. What has God done? What has He taught you? What has changed? Then look ahead. Ask God for strength to keep serving, no matter what the next season brings.

Let your home be marked by one clear truth: this family belongs to the Lord.

Discussion Questions

1. What does it mean for our home to serve the Lord?
2. What choices show who or what we are serving?
3. What one step will we take this week to serve God together?
4. How can we keep this commitment strong in the year ahead?

Family Prayer

Lord, we choose to serve You. This house belongs to You. Help us live in a way that honors You. Teach us to obey with joy, to repent quickly, and to love one another in truth. Strengthen us to follow You as a family. In Jesus' name. Amen.

Extra Chapter:
How to Make Family Bible Study Simple and Consistent

Practical Tips to Build a Lasting Habit in a Busy Home

Introduction: Start Where You Are

Family Bible study doesn't need to be long, complex, or perfect to be effective. Many parents feel pressure to "do it right," but the most important step is to **begin** and **keep going**. This chapter gives you clear, proven tips to make Bible study feel simple, natural, and consistent in your home, no matter your family size, schedule, or spiritual background.

1. Choose a Set Time and Stick With It

One of the biggest reasons families skip Bible study is lack of routine. If you're always deciding when to do it, you'll often decide not to. The solution is simple: **pick one time and protect it.**

- **Best times:** After dinner, before bed, or on Sunday evenings work for many families.

- **Consistency beats intensity:** Twenty minutes each week builds more than two hours once a month.

- **Put it on the calendar:** Treat this time like an appointment. Don't let it float.

You'll miss a week sometimes. That's okay. Just pick it up again the next week without guilt.

2. Keep It Short and Focused

Children and teens respond best to **clear structure and short sessions.** Don't aim for deep theology discussions or hour-long teaching. Keep your family's attention by keeping it simple:

- *5 minutes*: Read the Bible passage.

- **5–10 minutes:** Read the short lesson aloud (like the weekly chapters in this book).

- **10 minutes:** Ask questions and pray together.

The goal is **faithful rhythm**, not long performance.

3. Read Scripture Out Loud, Together

Let your family hear the Bible spoken with your voice and their own. This builds memory, reverence, and familiarity with God's Word. Here's how:

- Take turns reading verses if children are old enough.

- Read slowly and clearly.

- Always read the **Scripture verse first**, even before the lesson.

Reading out loud builds attention. It also shows your family that the Bible deserves full focus.

4. Keep a Bible in Your Meeting Space

Have one physical Bible set aside for your family study. Keep it in a visible, consistent place. This creates two helpful effects:

- It serves as a **visual reminder**.

- It removes the need to search for a Bible every week.

You might even use a highlighter to mark each weekly verse as you go. Over time, you'll see a visible trail of what your family has studied.

5. Let Everyone Speak, But Keep It Brief

Don't force long conversations. Simply ask one or two clear questions from the lesson and let each person share **one thought**. Then move on. This helps:

- Children feel safe speaking up.

- Teens avoid pressure to say "the right thing."

- Parents model humility by answering too.

The point is connection, not perfection.

6. Keep Prayer Short and Real

Long, formal prayers are not required. Family prayer should be simple, sincere, and short. Use this format:

- One person prays for the group.

- Or, each person says one sentence: "God, help me..." or "Thank You for..."

This keeps everyone engaged and avoids overthinking. If someone doesn't want to pray out loud, that's okay. Invite, but never force.

7. Involve Children with Small Tasks

Children like to contribute when they know what to do. Try assigning roles:

- One person reads the verse.

- One opens in prayer.

- One lights a candle or brings the Bible to the table.

- One writes down prayer requests.

This builds buy-in and helps them feel responsible.

8. Choose One Room for Bible Study

Don't move locations each time. Choose one spot:

- The dining table.
- The living room floor.
- A child's room with everyone gathered around.

This trains your family to connect that space with Bible time. Familiarity builds habit.

9. Remove Distractions

Phones and screens can quickly undo your effort. Here's how to prevent that:

- **No phones** at the table.
- Turn off the TV.
- Ask one parent to silence their device for the full time.

The goal is full attention. Even 15 minutes of focused time is better than an hour full of interruptions.

10. Make Missed Weeks No Big Deal

Life happens. Illness, travel, or conflict may cause a missed week. Don't try to double up or cram two weeks into one. **Skip ahead and continue.**

This communicates grace and perseverance. It teaches your family that spiritual growth is steady, not perfect.

11. Use Visual Cues to Reinforce the Habit

- Keep a paper chart where you check off each completed week.
- Use a small notebook to write one takeaway per session.
- Post your family's Bible verse of the week on the fridge.

Seeing progress helps children stay engaged. It also reminds the family that something meaningful is happening.

12. Let It Feel Like Real Life

Expect interruptions, silly comments, and imperfect answers. That's normal.

You might:

- Have toddlers squirming.
- Hear a child say, "I don't get it."
- Watch a teen look bored some weeks.

Don't scold or stress. Just keep going. Over time, they'll absorb far more than they show in the moment.

13. Use Your Real Tone, Not a "Religious Voice"

Speak in your normal voice. You don't need to sound like a teacher or preacher. Keep it:

- Calm.

- Honest.

- Direct.

Speak from your heart, and your children will listen.

14. Create a Family Scripture Memory Habit

You don't need to memorize long passages. Try one verse every few weeks. Post it in one place and say it together each day:

- In the car.

- At the table.

- During bedtime.

Repetition builds memory. It also trains the mind and anchors the heart.

15. Celebrate the Wins

Mark progress:

- Finished 10 weeks in a row? Do a special meal.

- Child asked a great question? Mention it with praise.

- Someone showed spiritual growth? Speak it out loud.

Recognition builds motivation. Celebrate effort, not perfection.

16. Use Music or Worship (Optional)

Some families enjoy a short worship song before or after study. If your children are musical, let them lead a song. If not, try:

- Playing one simple worship song at the beginning.

- Singing a short chorus or hymn.

This helps center the mind and slow the pace.

17. Model What You Want to See

Children learn most from what you do, not what you say. If you:

- Pray regularly,

- Confess when you're wrong,

- Speak Scripture into daily life,

Then your family will absorb those patterns.

Let your life teach, not just your words.

18. Keep Going Beyond the Book

Once you finish the 52 weeks, don't stop meeting. Use the same rhythm, but change the material. Ideas:

- Choose one book of the Bible and read one chapter per week.

- Ask each family member to pick a new verse each week.

- Revisit the 52-week study again with new discussion.

The goal is **ongoing spiritual rhythm**, not a one-time study.

Final Encouragement: You Don't Have to Be Perfect

You don't need special training. You don't need all the answers. You need a Bible, a plan, and a willingness to show up. God honors faithfulness. Your family doesn't need you to teach everything; they need you to create space for God's Word.

If you've made it through this book, you've already built something rare and lasting. Keep showing up. Keep trusting God to do the deep work. He is building something eternal in your home.

Checklist

This checklist is designed to support families who are using your book *52-Week Bible Study for Families Made Simple*, and want a repeatable framework they can apply **every single week**, even beyond the 52 chapters. It's broken into **10 core categories** with step-by-step actions, tips, and reminders. Each category includes weekly guidance to make family Bible study clear, repeatable, and low-pressure.

1. Prepare the Space

Why it matters: A consistent space creates familiarity. It helps everyone focus without starting from scratch each time.

Weekly checklist:

- Choose a quiet, comfortable room.
- Keep the space clean and ready ahead of time.
- Set out a physical Bible.
- Remove distractions (TV off, phones silenced).
- Place a visible reminder: verse card, calendar, notebook.

Tips:

- Use the same table or corner each week.
- Store everything in one basket or box labeled "Bible Study."

2. Pick a Regular Time

Why it matters: Families follow patterns. Without a regular time, Bible study can easily be pushed aside.

Weekly checklist:

- Choose a weekly day and time (e.g., Sunday after dinner).
- Let everyone know at least one day in advance.
- Write it on the family calendar.
- Treat it like a family commitment, not an option.
- Adjust only if truly necessary, and reschedule quickly.

Tips:

- Use reminders or alarms for older kids and teens.
- Keep a "missed week" mindset: Skip ahead, don't double up.

3. Read the Weekly Scripture Aloud

Why it matters: Scripture is the foundation. Reading it out loud builds reverence and familiarity.

Weekly checklist:

- Open the Bible before anything else.
- Read the week's verse clearly and slowly.
- Let children take turns reading if they're able.
- Ask: "What word or phrase stood out to you?"
- Highlight or underline the verse in your Bible.

Tips:

- Use one family Bible to mark your journey over time.
- Read the verse again at the end to reinforce it.

4. Read the Lesson Together

Why it matters: Lessons provide context and practical application. They keep families focused and clear.

Weekly checklist:

- Choose one person to read the chapter aloud.
- Allow children to follow along if they prefer.
- Pause if someone has a question, but don't get stuck.
- Keep it moving if attention starts to wander.
- Emphasize clarity, not performance.

Tips:

- If your child doesn't understand a sentence, simplify it.

- Keep tone natural, not "preachy."

5. Ask the Guided Discussion Questions

Why it matters: Talking about the Bible helps everyone process, reflect, and apply it.

Weekly checklist:

- Ask each question from the chapter out loud.

- Let each person share at least one thought.

- Keep answers brief and respectful, no teasing.

- Thank each person for their answer.

- Parents answer, too; model humility and honesty.

Tips:

- If a child says "I don't know," ask, "What do you think it might mean?"

- Don't pressure silence. Sometimes thinking is the answer.

6. Pray Together

Why it matters: Prayer connects your family to God. It builds spiritual closeness and trust.

Weekly checklist:

- Ask, "Who wants to pray today?"

- Give the option to pray one sentence each.

- If no one wants to pray aloud, one adult can pray for all.

- Include requests that came up in the discussion.

- End by thanking God for His Word.

Tips:

- Keep it short.

- Avoid "perfect-sounding" language. Simple is best.

7. Record Your Progress

Why it matters: Tracking creates momentum. It reminds you that small steps are adding up.

Weekly checklist:

- Mark off the week on a printed tracker or chart.
- Write the verse reference in a visible place (fridge, chalkboard, whiteboard).
- Have one child add the date and verse to a "Faith Journal."
- Review a few past weeks to celebrate consistency.
- Keep a running prayer list or answered prayer journal.

Tips:

- Use checkmarks, stickers, or stamps for young children.
- Take a photo once a month to document your journey.

8. Apply the Lesson During the Week

Why it matters: Bible study is not just about reading. It's about transformation.

Weekly checklist:

- Pick one application challenge from the chapter.
- Ask each person: "What is one thing you'll do differently this week?"
- Review this the next time you meet.
- Speak the week's verse during relevant moments.
- Support each other when a challenge comes up.

Tips:

- Use the verse to guide decisions ("Let's be patient, like we talked about in Bible study").
- Turn conflict into a reminder of what you studied.

9. Make Room for Questions and Wonder

Why it matters: Curiosity leads to growth. Faith becomes real when space is made for questions.

Weekly checklist:

- Ask, "Did anyone have a question about this week's topic?"
- Listen fully without jumping to correct.
- If you don't know, say, "Let's look it up together."
- Write down hard questions for deeper study.
- Return to big questions in future weeks.

Tips:

- Don't be afraid of doubt.
- Even off-topic questions are signs your children are thinking.

10. Keep the Atmosphere Calm and Consistent

Why it matters: Atmosphere affects memory. A calm, focused setting builds stronger spiritual habits.

Weekly checklist:

- Keep your tone calm and patient, even if kids fidget.
- Don't allow sarcasm or frustration during study.
- Keep expectations realistic; children will not always sit still.
- End with encouragement, not pressure.
- Thank your family for showing up.

Tips:

- After studying, affirm your child's effort: "I liked how you shared your thoughts today."
- If the mood was tense, say, "Let's reset and try again next week."

Optional Weekly Extras (Choose 1–2)

- Sing one short worship song before or after study.
- Memorize a verse as a family over several weeks.
- Write a letter of encouragement to someone and include a verse.
- Watch a short Bible-based video related to the topic.
- Use a Bible map or illustration to give context.
- Share a personal story of when this week's verse helped you.

Final Reflection Questions for Parents (Optional)

- What stood out to me in this week's study?
- Did I model peace and patience?
- What habit is helping our Bible study most?
- Where do we need to simplify or refocus?
- What spiritual growth do I see in my children?

Conclusion: The Goal is Faithfulness, Not Perfection

This checklist is not about checking boxes. It's about making room for God to shape your home. You will miss a week. You'll forget a task. Someone will interrupt with a silly comment or a sibling squabble. That doesn't mean it's not working.

What matters is that you return.

When you do, God honors that faithfulness. Over time, your family's pattern of meeting, reading, praying, and applying Scripture will leave a mark. Not just on your calendar, but on your hearts.

Check out another book in the series

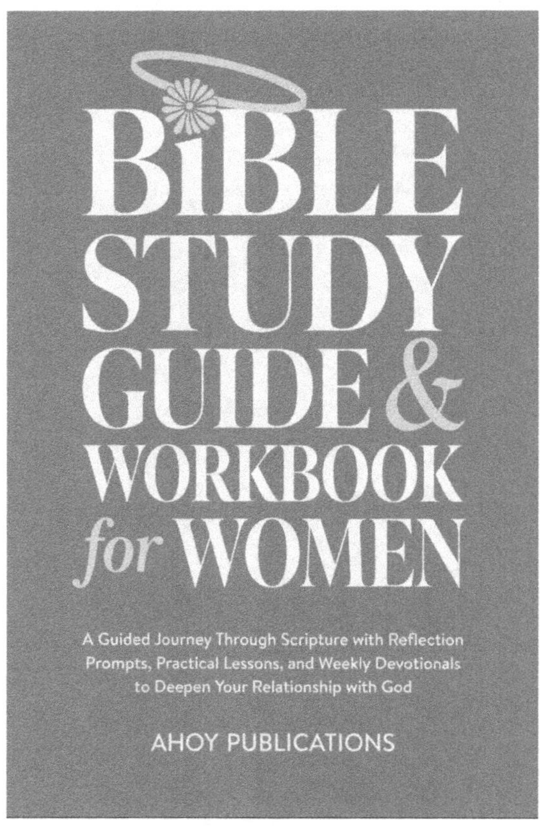

Welcome Aboard, Check Out This Limited-Time Free Bonus!

Ahoy, reader! Welcome to the Ahoy Publications family, and thanks for snagging a copy of this book! Since you've chosen to join us on this journey, we'd like to offer you something special.

Check out the link below for a FREE e-book filled with delightful facts about American History.

But that's not all - you'll also have access to our exclusive email list with even more free e-books and insider knowledge. Well, what are ye waiting for? Click the link below to join and set sail toward exciting adventures in American History.

Access your bonus here

https://ahoypublications.com/

Or, Scan the QR code!